SAN SEBASTIÁN

TOP EXPERIENCES · LOCAL LIFE

CATHERINE LE NEVEZ

Contents

Plan Your Trip

San Sebastián's Playa de la Concha (p122)
ALEXANDER DEMYANENKO/SHUTTERSTOCK ©

COVID-19

We have re-checked every business in this book before publication to ensure that it is still open after the COVID-19 outbreak. However, the economic and social impacts of COVID-19 will continue to be felt long after the outbreak has been contained. Therefore many businesses, services and events referenced in this guide may experience ongoing restrictions. Some businesses may be temporarily closed, or have changed their opening hours and services; some unfortunately could have closed permanently. We suggest you check with venues before visiting for the latest information.

Bilbao & San Sebastián's Top Experiences

Explore the iconic Museo Guggenheim Bilbao (p50)

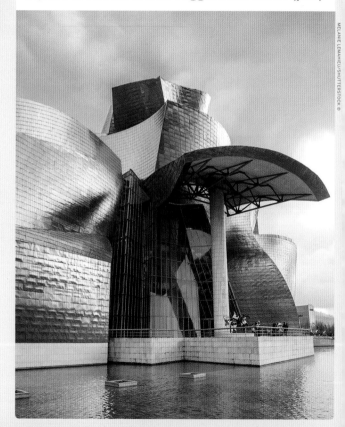

MELANIE LEMAHIEU/SHUTTERSTOCK ©

Admire fine art at Museo de Bellas Artes (p54)

Understand the past at Gernika (p86)

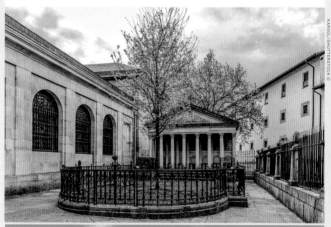

KARSOL/SHUTTERSTOCK ©

FRANCESCO BONINO/SHUTTERSTOCK ©

Discover Coastal Basque lifestyle in Getaria (p90)

Delve into Basque culture and society at San Telmo Museoa (p104)

HERACLES KRITIKOS/SHUTTERSTOCK ©

Enter an aquatic wonderland at Aquarium (p106)

Hit the beach at Playa de la Concha (p122)

Enjoy mountaintop views at Monte Igueldo (p124)

Dining Out

The Basque Country is famous the world over for its cuisine. Whether you're stopping for a glass of wine and a few bite-sized pintxos at a local bar in Bilbao, San Sebastián or a coastal village, or savouring cutting-edge gastronomy at a Michelin-starred restaurant, you're bound to have a memorable food experience.

Pintxos

Enter any bar in the region and the counter is sure to be groaning under the weight of a small mountain of tiny plates of culinary art. These are *pintxos* (Basque tapas; pictured), which will redefine your interpretation of the bar snack.

Basque Cuisine

The Basque Coast gives rise to superb seafood dishes, such as *bacalao al pil-pil* (salted cod and garlic in an olive-oil emul-

sion) and *chipirones en su tinta* (baby squid in its own ink), while the lush hills and mountains are the source of *chuleton de buey* (steaks – invariably massive).

Best Pintxos

La Cuchara de San Telmo Arguably one of the best *pintxo* bars in San Sebastián. (p109)

Bergara Bar The pick of the *pintxo* bars in San Sebastián's Gros district. (p144)

La Viña del Ensanche Go for the tasting menu at Bilbao's standout *pintxo* bar. (p62)

Best Basque

Casa Victor Montes Bilbao landmark with exquisite *pintxos* and prized steaks. (p39)

Gastroteka Danontzat A fun spot in the centre of Hondarribia. (p152)

Tamarises Izarra Contemporary Basque cuisine in Getxo. (p82)

Bascook High-end culinary wizardry set in an atmospheric former Bilbao salt warehouse. (p63)

Bodegón Alejandro Elegant cellar restaurant in San Sebastián. (p114)

Rio-Oja Stews are among the classics at this Bilbao favourite. (p40)

ALFERNEC/SHUTTERSTOCK ©

Best Seafood

Mesón Arropain Magnificent fish plates and seafood appetisers in Lekeitio. (p96)

Elkano Famed seafood served up in the coastal village of Getaria. (p91)

Casa Cámara Set out over the water, with a live-seafood cage lowered through the floor. (p153)

El Puertito Slurp down oysters and sip crisp white wine at this garrulous den near Bilbao's stadium. (p63)

Kata 4 Top spot for feasting on seafood in San Sebastián's new town. (p133)

Karola Etxea Dine on fresh seafood in a former fishing village above Getxo's Puerto Viejo. (p82)

Best International

Basquery Contemporary flavours in Bilbao's new town pair with the in-house brews. (p64)

Gerald's Bar San Sebastián outpost of a Melbourne restaurant with an international palate. (p144)

Worth a Trip: Michelin Star Tour

With 29 Michelin stars, the Basque Country is a gourmet's nirvana. Fifteen stars are in and around San Sebastián, including the following once-in-a-lifetime experiences.

Arzak (www.arzak.es) Three stars; 3.5km east of San Sebastián.

Martín Berasategui (www.martinberasategui. com) Three stars; 9km southwest of San Sebastián.

Mugaritz (www.mugaritz.com) Two stars; 10km southeast of San Sebastián.

Bilbao & San Sebastián on a Plate
Pintxos

Artful touches transform the *pintxo* into a delicacy

Careful cooking illustrates the Basque quest for perfection

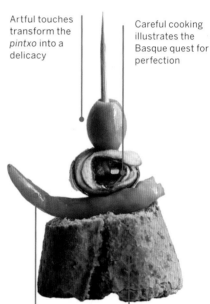

High-quality ingredients are the cornerstone of great *pintxos*

Freshly baked baguette-style bread forms the base of many *pintxos*

★ Top Five for Pintxos

La Viña del Ensanche (p62) A Bilbao classic since 1927.

Gure-Toki (p39) Top choice on Bilbao's Plaza Nueva.

La Cuchara deSan Telmo (p109) One of San Sebastián's best *pinxto* bars.

Casa Urola (p114) San Sebastián stalwart with hams hanging overhead.

Txalupa Gastroleku (p109) San Sebastián specialist with a boat-shaped bar.

Pintxos in the Basque Country

A showcase for the Basque Country's bountiful produce, *pintxos* come in limitless varieties, incorporating grilled prawns, plump anchovies, cod, tender squid, spider crab, juicy stuffed peppers, wild mushrooms, Idiazabal cheese, air-dried ham, earthy *morcilla* (blood sausage) and much more. Wherever you go, expect deliciously inventive fare, as creativity is a hallmark of these Basque delicacies.

Gure-Toki (p39)

FORSBERG/SHUTTERSTOCK ©

Bar Open

While the Basque Country may not be famous for its nightlife, there's a lot happening if you know where to look. You'll find a mix of buzzing cafes, convivial wine bars and lovely shaded terraces. Later on, you can join the party-minded crowds at bars, nightclubs and live music joints, with the revelry continuing late into the night.

Live Music & Culture

San Sebastián and Bilbao have an array of impressive venues that play a central role in their cultural life. Jazz, classical music, dance performances, live theatre, film screenings and opera are all part of the mix. The vibe is generally friendly and easy-going with a welcome lack of pretension. Venues' websites have details of upcoming gigs and performances.

Best Bars

Mala Gissona Beer House A lively local spot that serves the best craft brews in Gros. (p145)

La Gintonería Donostiarra Gin fans raise a glass at this G&T-loving Gros joint. (p146)

Bar Ondarra The best place to head after a day on Playa de la Zurriola. (p146)

Pokhara One of the top places to start the night (or early afternoon) in San Sebastián's new town. (p135)

El Balcón de la Lola Bilbao's go-to late-night spot with a dance floor that draws in the party people. (p67)

Residence Catch live music or just stop in for a drink with a laid-back Bilbao crowd. (p66)

Best Old-School Spots

Museo del Whisky San Sebastián bar with a museum's worth of whisky and whisky paraphernalia. (p135)

Côte Bar An easy-going drinking den in San Sebastián's old town. (p116)

Bataplan Disco Get your groove on at this classic DJ-fuelled spot near Playa de la Concha. (p134)

Best Cafes

Koh Tao Slow down over a coffee or cool drink at this friendly San Sebastián cafe. (p136)

Baobab Riverside Bilbao cafe with regular jam sessions, poetry readings and an art-centric vibe. (p66)

FRANCESCO BONINO/SHUTTERSTOCK ©

Bohemian Lane The best place to linger over an organic juice or coffee and dessert in Bilbao's old town. (p43)

Best Performing Arts

Kursaal San Sebastián's architecturally striking performing arts venue stages an impressive cultural line-up. (p146)

Teatro Victoria Eugenia Dating from 1912, this is a lavish San Sebastián theatre to catch a performance. (pictured; p136)

Tabakalera Celebrated San Sebastián cultural centre with a line-up of film screenings and concerts. (p146)

Teatro Arriaga Take in a classical music concert in the neobaroque surrounds of Bilbao's beautiful old town theatre. (p43)

Euskalduna Palace Enjoy classical music from Bilbao's two orchestras in this striking building. (p69)

Best Live Music

Kafe Antzokia The vibrant heart of Bilbao's contemporary Basque culture: music, public discussions (in Basque), a cafe and bar. (p68)

Altxerri Jazz Bar A San Sebastián temple to jazz and blues, hosting local and international musicians. (p118)

Le Bukowski One of San Sebastián's best places to hear eclectic bands from soul to rock. (p146)

Etxekalte Live jazz, experimental sounds and DJs near the waterfront in San Sebastián. (p118)

Bilborock Bilbao's concert venue for rock and metal lovers occupies an imaginatively converted 17th-century church. (p69)

Bilbao & San Sebastián in a Glass
Txakoli

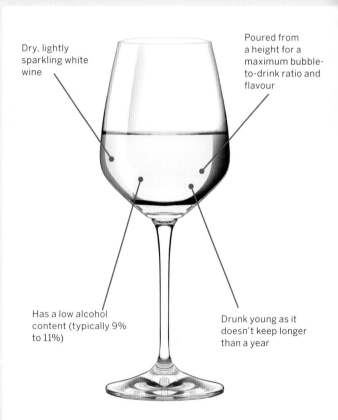

Dry, lightly sparkling white wine

Poured from a height for a maximum bubble-to-drink ratio and flavour

Has a low alcohol content (typically 9% to 11%)

Drunk young as it doesn't keep longer than a year

★ Top Five for Txakoli

Elkano Txakoli (p98) Near Zarautz, this 1830-established, sixth-generation winery runs tours and tastings.

Cork (p65) Bilbao wine bar run by a former Basque sommelier champion.

Vinoteka Ardoka (p154) Contemporary Hondarribia wine bar.

Rojo y Negro (p133) *Pintxo* bar in San Sebastián serving a *txakoli* sangria.

La Bendita (p47) Pick up bottles to take home at this Bilbao gourmet shop.

Txakoli in the Basque Country

An aperitif that pairs perfectly with *pintxos*, txakoli (tcha-koh-*lee*) comes from three renowned districts. The most highly regarded is grown near Getaria, with vines covering the southeast-facing slopes just inland of the town. This wine has a very pale yellow to greenish colour. The other *txakoli*-producing regions are Bizkaia (Biscay Province), around Bilbao, and Álava, to Bilbao's south.

Grapes used to make *txakoli*

ASIFE/SHUTTERSTOCK ©

Treasure Hunt

The Basque Country has an enticing array of regional wares, locally made fashions and gourmet shops. The best places for indie stores and foodie spots are in the historic neighbourhoods of Bilbao (Casco Viejo) and San Sebastián (Parte Vieja). Elsewhere, you'll find a wide mix of small boutiques and brand-name favourites.

MARK READ/ACQUIA ©

Best Basque Gifts & Souvenirs

Perfumería Benegas Sample perfumes, including its house creations, inside this long-running San Sebastián perfumery. (p137)

Alboka Artesanía One-of-a-kind Basque handicrafts from a little shop on San Sebastián's Plaza de la Constitución. (p119)

DendAZ All-Basque designers showcase their works in Bilbao. (p70)

Best Food & Drink

Mimo San Sebastián Gourmet Shop One of the best places in town to pick up high-quality food and wine. (p138)

Mercado de la Bretxa San Sebastián's central market is packed with culinary treasures. (pictured; p119)

Mercado de la Ribera This is where Bilbao's top chefs buy their ingredients. (p46)

Aitor Lasa Small but well-stocked San Sebastián food shop with all the essentials for a memorable picnic. (p119)

La Quesaría Aromatic little cheese (and wine) shop in Bilbao's old town. (p45)

La Bendita Bilbao gourmet shop with wines, olive oils and other edibles by small Basque Country producers. (p47)

Almacen Coloniales y Bacalao Gregorio Martín For 80 years this Bilbao boutique has been selling only the finest *bacalao* (salted cod). (p47)

Best Fashion & Accessories

Ätakontu Graphic T-shirts by Bilbao textile artists. (p43)

Gorostiga *Txapelas* (Basque berets) in Bilbao. (p46)

Peletería Ramón Ezkerra Leather handcrafted into trend-setting fashions in Bilbao. (p45)

Pukas Browse the latest beachwear at this San Sebastián surf specialist. (p118)

Loreak Mendian This Basque label has an excellent variety of men's and women's apparel in San Sebastián. (p138)

Museums & Public Art

NITO/SHUTTERSTOCK ©

Aside from the famed Museo Guggenheim Bilbao, the Basque Country is home to an outstanding collection of cultural treasures. You can also learn about the Basque people, their language and ancient traditions at regional museums covering history, archaeology and maritime lore.

Best Art Museums & Sculptures

Museo Guggenheim Bilbao Landmark museum flanked by iconic sculptures including Jeff Koons' floral *Puppy* and hosting superb exhibitions. (p50)

Museo de Bellas Artes An enchanting Bilbao museum to explore Basque artists, as well as heavy hitters from other parts of Spain. (p54)

San Telmo Museoa San Sebastián's overview of Basque culture through the ages, including impressive contemporary art from Basque painters. (p104)

Peine del Viento This iron and pink granite sculpture has become a symbol of San Sebastián. (p134)

Construcción Vacía The brooding *Empty Space* sculpture sits below San Sebastián's Monte Urgull. (p113)

Statue of Christ Monte Urgull is topped by a monumental statue of Christ that's dramatically floodlit at night. (p111)

Best Basque History & Culture Museums

Euskal Museoa In Bilbao, the world's most complete museum of Basque history and culture. (p37)

Arkeologi Museo Bilbao museum reveals just how long the Basques have lived in this neck of the woods. (pictured; p38)

Museo de la Paz de Gernika An often heart-wrenching but thought-provoking museum of war and peace. (p87)

Cristóbal Balenciaga Museoa Browse exquisite couture pieces designed by Basque designer Cristóbal Balenciaga in his hometown, Getaria. (p91)

Best Maritime History Museums

Itsasmuseum Set sail on the seven seas at Bilbao's high-tech maritime museum. (p60)

Albaola Foundation A charming maritime museum housed in a former Pasaia boatyard. (p153)

Architecture

ANDI111/SHUTTERSTOCK ©

Welcome to one of Europe's architecturally daring corners. Here you'll find the grand, the modern and the genre-changing. While a walk around any Basque city will reveal a cauldron of architectural styles, it's Bilbao that leads the way with bold works by Frank Gehry, Santiago Calatrava and Philippe Starck among others.

Best Contemporary Buildings

Museo Guggenheim Bilbao Visit throughout the day to admire the play of light on the titanium shell. (p50)

Azkuna Zentroa (Alhóndiga) Multitasking Philippe Starck creation with cinemas, a rooftop swimming pool, cafes and restaurants in Bilbao. (p60)

Kursaal San Sebastián's beloved modernist work, the Kursaal cultural centre represents two beached rocks. (p146)

Estadio San Mamés Bilbao's state-of-the-art football stadium is a city landmark. (p67)

Best Historic Buildings

San Telmo Museoa Partially housed in a 16th-century convent, this San Sebastián museum also incorporates a modern extension. (p104)

Ayuntamiento A casino in the 19th century, San Sebastián's town hall is still opulent today. (p132)

Universidad de Deusto This Bilbao landmark was designed by architect Francisco de Cubas in 1886 to house the Jesuit university. (p66)

Concordia Train Station Built in Bilbao in 1902, featuring a handsome art-nouveau facade of wrought iron and tiles. (pictured; p57)

Castillo de Carlos V Strategically positioned on the hilltop of Hondarribia's old town, this castle is today a hotel. (p152)

Hotel Maria Cristina San Sebastián's most palatial hotel defines belle époque splendour. (p130)

Best Bridges

Puente Colgante The first-ever transporter bridge is a remarkable feat of engineering and a Unesco World Heritage Site in Portugalete. (p78)

Zubizuri The dazzling 1997-built 'White Bridge' by Santiago Calatrava helped transform Bilbao's cityscape. (p61)

Puente de Maria Cristina Walk under the watchful eyes of angels on this belle époque bridge in San Sebastián. (p131)

For Free

One of the delights of Bilbao, San Sebastián and the Basque Country is that many of the more enjoyable sights and activities won't break the bank. In fact, they're often completely free – as are all of the region's beaches, markets, walking trails and plethora of picnic spots.

FLAREZT/SHUTTERSTOCK ©

Best Free Cultural Sights

Koldo Mitxelena Kulturunea This free cultural centre in San Sebastián hosts innovative exhibitions. (p130)

Casa de la Historia Atop Monte Urgull, this small gallery provides an intriguing glimpse into Basque history. (p112)

Best Free Outdoor Experiences

Parque de Doña Casilda de Iturrizar The most beautiful park in Bilbao is whimsical, flowery and completely free. (pictured; p61)

Monte Urgull Be king of the castle at the top of Monte Urgull and enjoy stellar views over San Sebastián. (p111)

Parque de Cristina Enea San Sebastián's prettiest green space makes an enticing setting for a stroll. (p143)

Playa de la Concha Spending a day on San Sebastián's most famous beach doesn't cost anything (ice cream aside). (p122)

Las Siete Calles One of the most pleasant ways of exploring is strolling streets such as Bilbao's seven atmospheric lanes. (p37)

Isla de San Nicolás During low tide, it's good fun to walk out to this tiny island overlooking Lekeitio. (p96)

Top Tips Saving Money

○ Many museums and galleries in the region offer free entry one day a week.

○ The region's multitude of festivals (p44) are often free.

○ Students and seniors should bring ID and flash it at every opportunity for reduced prices.

For Kids

ANDREW BABBLE/SHUTTERSTOCK ©

Hands-on museums, boat and funicular rides, and lovely beaches and parks set the stage for a memorable family holiday in the family-friendly Basque Country, which has activities galore to inspire and amuse travellers of all ages.

Itsasmuseum Seafaring adventures await in Bilbao's stimulating maritime museum. (p60)

Aquarium Smile at the sharks and pet the blennies in San Sebastián's underwater world. (p106)

Funicular de Artxanda Bilbao's clanky funicular railway is a hit with children of all ages. (pictured; p61)

Isla de Santa Clara Take a boat ride out to Isla de Santa Clara off San Sebastián. (p113)

Monte Igueldo Funfair rides, ice cream and a funicular railway keep kids happy in San Sebastián. (p124)

Playa de Ondarreta Calm seas, volleyball nets and sandcastles on this San Sebastián beach. (p130)

Albaola Foundation See a 16th-century whaling ship being built in Pasaia. (p153)

Cuevas de Santimamiñe Delve into this cave system outside of Gernika. (p87)

Plaza del Solar Dance to Sunday concerts on the Portugalete waterfront. (p78)

Castillo de la Mota Play king of the castle atop the summit overlooking San Sebastián. (p111)

Faro de Santa Catalina Get a taste of seafaring life on a boat simulator in Lekeitio. (p96)

Basque Coast Geopark Peer back in time a few million years on a walk or boat tour from Zumaia. (p98)

Top Tips For Children

○ Most restaurants welcome kids, although children's menus, high chairs and changing facilities are rare.

○ Reserve baby cots when booking your hotel as numbers are often limited.

○ Nappies (diapers) and formula are available at *farmacias* (pharmacies).

Active Bilbao & San Sebastián

A renowned destination for surfing, the Basque Country has reliable waves all year round. Other water sports, such as kayaking and SUP (stand-up paddleboarding) are also popular, as is hiking along the spectacular coastline and in the hilly hinterland.

ALVARO GERMAN VILELA/SHUTTERSTOCK ©

Best Surf Schools

Pukas Surf Eskola Ride San Sebastián's superb surf with Pukas. (p143)

Mundaka Surf Shop Hit Mundaka's fabled waves with this surf school. (p94)

Moor Surf Eskola Zarautz surf school overlooking the beach. (p98)

Best Aquatic Activities

River Cheer Explore Bilbao's waterways in your own four-person boat. (p60)

Bilbobentura Join an organised paddle or hire a kayak or SUP in Bilbao. (p60)

Kayak Basque Country Take a kayaking or fishing trip from Hondarribia. (p152)

Sokaire Activities offered by this Central Basque Coast outfit include 'coasteering' expeditions. (p95)

Best Walking

Basque Coast Geopark Trails of varying lengths let you explore the coast's extraordinary geology. (p98)

San Sebastián to Pasaia Hike the 7.7km coastal trail, part of the Camino del Norte, linking Gros with Pasaia. (p145)

Paseo de Punta Galea Coastal walking path around the Punta Galea headland north of Getxo. (p84)

Top Tips For Surfing

○ Surf webcams and forecasts are available at www.magicseaweed.com and www.surfline.com.

○ Average water temperatures range from 12°C in February/March to 22°C in August.

○ Surf schools typically cater for all skill levels, and hire equipment (including wetsuits).

Beaches

ALBERTO LOYO/SHUTTERSTOCK ©

The Basque Country's spectacular coastline ranges from tiny, rocky coves hidden down bumpy tracks to world-famous urban strands. For real fun, take a slow drive along the coast allowing time to find your own favourite hidden patch of sand.

Playa de la Concha Among the world's most beautiful, San Sebastián's city beach graces countless postcards. (p122)

Playa de la Zurriola San Sebastián's surf beach par excellence. (p143)

Playa de Ondarreta Gorgeous sweep of San Sebastián sand. (pictured; p130)

Lekeitio During low tide, you can stroll from the sands out to the Isla de San Nicolás. (p96)

Playa de Hondarribia Calm waters make this family-friendly beach a prime swimming spot for young kids. (p151)

Hendaye A quick ferry ride from Hondarribia, this French beauty has a lovely stretch of shoreline. (p154)

Playa de Ereaga Getxo's sheltered sandy strip is just a metro ride away from downtown Bilbao. (p80)

Playa de Arrigunaga This Getxo beach sees offshore surf and on-shore skater action. (p75)

Playa de Laida Paddle out from Mundaka to these golden sands and surf breaks beyond. (p94)

Zarautz This small coastal village backs onto the region's longest swath of sand. (p98)

Top Tips

● Tides vary greatly in the Basque Country, and broad stretches of sand can quickly be swallowed up by the incoming waters.

● Most beaches are patrolled by lifeguards in July and August; at other times, check locally to ensure conditions are safe for swimming.

● Sunbathing topless is acceptable on all beaches; tourist offices can advise on beaches where nudist sunbathing is permitted.

Under the Radar Bilbao & San Sebastián

JORGE ARGAZKIAK/SHUTTERSTOCK ©

Bilbao and San Sebastián are renowned for big-hitting attractions like the gleaming Museo Guggenheim Bilbao and storied beaches such as Playa de la Concha, but there's plenty to discover off the beaten track, whether exploring the cities, forested hinterland or along the beautiful Basque coast.

Explore Local Neighbourhoods

Until the COVID-19 pandemic impacted international travel, the Basque Country received some 3.4 million visitors annually. Many descend on the narrow streets of the cities' old towns, Bilbao's Casco Viejo and San Sebastián's Parte Vieja. Venturing beyond them brings you to intriguing areas like medieval Portugalete and the municipality of Getxo, with sandy beaches, scenic waterfront paths and traditional seafood restaurants in Bilbao, and the backstreets of San Sebastián's New Town and cool, young seaside neighbourhood Gros, with great shops, eateries and lively local hangouts.

Best Under-the-Radar Sights & Activities

Parque de Cristina Enea (p143) Stroll the wooded paths and lawns of this loved San Sebastián park.

River Cheer (p60) Cruise along the Nervión past Bilbao's landmarks by renting your own four-person aluminium boat.

Crusoe Treasure (p94) Head out to sea to sample wines from the world's first underwater winery or try them on shore.

Arrantzaleen Museoa (p93) Understand the importance of Basque fishing over the centuries at Bermeo's Arrantzaleen Museoa.

Best Under-the-Radar Beaches

Playa de Murgita (p145) Cool off mid-hike at this hidden beach located between San Sebastián and Pasaia.

Playa de Ereaga (p80) Laze on a sunbed at this favourite with Bilbao families in Gexto.

Playa de Itzurun (p98) Spot ammonites and other fossils among cliffs at Zumaia's western beach (pictured).

Four Perfect Days

Day 1

MAURICE ROUGEMONT/GETTY IMAGES ©

Stroll along Bilbao's river, stopping at Santiago Calatrava's eye-catching **Zubizuri** (p61). Continue to the **Museo Guggenheim Bilbao** (p50), allowing time to admire the exterior and surrounding sculptures. For lunch, feast on Basque delicacies at **La Viña del Ensanche** (p62).

Walk through dreamy **Parque de Doña Casilda de Iturrizar** (p61) and on to **Museo de Bellas Artes** (p54) for Bilbao's best collection of Basque and Spanish artists. Continue to **Euskal Museoa** (p37) for a Basque history lesson.

In the evening wander through the Casco Viejo, grazing on *pintxos* at **Casa Victor Montes** (pictured; p39) and enjoying drinks and live music at **Kafe Antzokia** (p68).

Day 2

CHRISTIAN KOBER/ACQUIA ©

Skip the motorway to San Sebastián, and instead take a slow, spectacular drive along the undulating coast road. Visit Portugalete's Unesco-listed **Puente Colgante** (p78), then head east to the jaw-dropping **San Juan de Gaztelugatxe** (p93).

For lunch, make your way to **Lekeitio** (p95) for a seafood feast, then take a siesta on the sublime beachfront (pictured). If the tide is low, walk out to the **Isla de San Nicolás** (p96).

Continue to seaside **Getaria** (p91), strolling its picturesque lanes before viewing the exquisite designs of the town's most famous son at the **Cristóbal Balenciaga Museoa** (p91). As the day cools, make for the world-renowned *pintxo* bars of San Sebastián.

Day 3

Start with a crash course in Basque culture at **San Telmo Museoa** (pictured; p104), check out the living exhibits in the city's stellar **Aquarium** (p106), then climb nearby **Monte Urgull** (p111) for magnificent city views.

For lunch, sample fried fish by the harbour or legendary *pintxos* in the old town. Afterwards, worship the sun on San Sebastián's near-perfect beaches: try **Playa de la Concha** (p122) for gentle waves or **Playa de la Zurriola** (p143) for surf.

In the early evening, explore Gros' indie boutiques, cafes, and *pintxo* bars along Calle de Peña y Goñi. End the night with a concert at the **Kursaal** (p146) or with drinks and live music at **Le Bukowski** (p147).

Day 4

Today, head out of San Sebastián. Kick off in Pasaia, a short bus ride from town (or better yet a three-hour hike). Explore the area's whaling history at **Albaola Foundation** (p153) and visit Victor Hugo's holiday home, now **Casa Museo Victor Hugo** (pictured; p153). Lunch at **Casa Cámara** (p153).

Push on to Hondarribia's photogenic walled centre, the **Casco Histórico** (p151). For a change of scene, check out the town's seafront promenade and, weather permitting, swim at the sheltered **beach** (p151).

Spend the evening on **Calle San Pedro** (p151), Hondarribia's prettiest, liveliest street. Buzzing *pintxo* bar **Gran Sol** (p154) is a great place to start.

Need to Know

For detailed information, see Survival Guide (p159)

Currency
Euro (€)

Language
Spanish (Castilian) & Basque.

Visas
Not required for EU or Schengen country citizens. Other nationals need ETIAS pre-authorisation; some require a Schengen visa.

Money
ATMs widely available. Credit cards accepted in most hotels and restaurants.

Mobile Phones
Widely available local SIM cards can be used in compatible unlocked phones.

Time
Central European Time (GMT/UTC plus one hour)

Tipping
Not required, but rounding up is common.

Daily Budget

Budget: Less than €100
Dorm bed: €15–20; *hostal* (budget hotel) and *pensión* (guesthouse) double: €50–80

Multicourse *menú del día* lunch: €10–13

Glass of cider/beer/wine from: €1–2

Midrange: €100–200
Double room in midrange hotel: €80–160

Lunch/dinner in decent restaurants: €15–30

Cocktail: €8–14

Top end: More than €200
Double room in top-end hotel from: €160

Michelin-starred tasting menu from: €80

Advance Planning

Three months before Book accommodation.
Two months before Book high-end restaurants.
One week before Book tours and concert tickets.

Useful Websites

Lonely Planet (www.lonelyplanet.com/spain) Information, bookings and reviews.

Basque Country (www.basquecountry-tourism.com) Regional authority.

San Sebastián Turismo (www.sansebastian turismo.com) City authority.

Bilbao Turismo (www.bilbaoturismo.net) City authority.

Arriving in Bilbao & San Sebastián

Three airports serve this region: Bilbao (pictured), San Sebastián (domestic) and Biarritz, near San Sebastián in France.

✈ From Bilbao Airport

Buses run every 15 to 30 minutes to central Bilbao (€3, 20 minutes), stopping at Plaza de Federico Moyúa and the Intermodal bus station.

Taxis from the airport to the city centre cost €25 to €35.

Buses to San Sebastián (€17.10, 1¼ hours, hourly) run directly from Bilbao's airport.

✈ From San Sebastián Airport

Buses E20 and E21 run hourly to San Sebastián (€2.65, 30 minutes), stopping at Plaza de Gipuzkoa.

Taxis to the city centre cost €35 to €45.

✈ From Biarritz Airport

Buses link this airport in France with San Sebastián (€7, 45 minutes, up to eight daily).

Getting Around

Ⓜ Bilbao Metro

Bilbao's two metro lines meet at Sarriko. The most useful stations are Moyúa, Abando and Casco Viejo. Trains run every few minutes from 6am until 11pm (to 2am Fridays, all night Saturdays).

🚃 Bilbao Tram

Bilbao's modern tram system runs from the Atxuri train station to La Casilla. Key stops include the Guggenheim, Teatro Arriaga and the Intermodal bus station.

🚌 Bus

Bilbobus runs Bilbao-wide bus services, although most places of visitor interest are within walking distance of one another. In compact San Sebastián, bus 16 from the city centre to Monte Igueldo is the most useful line for visitors.

Bilbao Neighbourhoods

Bilbao New Town (p49)

Bilbao's new town has a diverse mix of architectural styles, food and shopping, worldclass galleries and attention-grabbing sights

Bilbao Old Town (Casco Viejo; p33)

A wanderer's delight, with attractive plazas, historic buildings and winding lanes. Come here for fabulous Basque food and fascinating cultural museums.

Museo Guggenheim Bilbao

Museo de Bellas Artes

Getxo & Portugalete (p73)

Just outside Bilbao and joined by the Unesco-listed Puente Colgante, Getxo and Portugalete have scenic waterfronts and excellent seafood restaurants.

Explore
Bilbao

*Bilbao is infused with a seafaring history and proudly inde-
pendent Basque spirit. In a glorious forest-fringed corner
of northwestern Spain, it has an enchanting Old Town
made up of narrow laneways and photogenic squares. It
is also home to dramatic contemporary architecture and
some fascinating museums.*

Bilbao Old Town (Casco Viejo)

The compact Casco Viejo, Bilbao's atmospheric old quarter, is full of charming streets, quirky shops, lively bars and fabulous cuisine. At the old town's heart are Bilbao's original seven streets, Las Siete Calles, which date from the 14th century.

The Short List

○ **Euskal Museoa (p37)** *Learning about the Basques, from ancient days to the present, at this repository of cultural treasures.*

○ **Plaza Nueva (p35)** *Taking in the beauty of the old town's photogenic 19th-century square.*

○ **Arkeologi Museo (p38)** *Strolling through the ages amid Neolithic carvings, Roman statuary and Middle Age finery.*

○ **Las Siete Calles (p37)** *Exploring the cobblestone lanes of Bilbao's oldest quarter.*

○ **Catedral de Santiago (p38)** *Checking out Bilbao's most important religious site, a Gothic Revival beauty dating back to the 1300s.*

Getting There & Around

Ⓜ The Casco Viejo station is close to the Plaza Nueva and the museums.

🚊 The Arriaga tram stop is by the Teatro Arriaga on the edge of the old town.

🏃 From the Museo Guggenheim, cross the river, turn right, and walk along the river to the Plaza del Arenal and the old town.

Neighbourhood Map on p36

Plaza Nueva (p35) JAM TRAVELS/SHUTTERSTOCK ©

Walking Tour 🥾

Bar-Hopping in Bilbao

One of the true highlights of a visit to Bilbao is the simple pleasure of savouring an oaky Rioja and nibbling on an artful pintxo in one of the city's many bars. This food- and drink-drenched route sees you hop from bar to bar, sipping wine and deliberating over which one serves the finest food.

Walk Facts

Start Plaza Nueva; Ⓜ Casco Viejo

Finish Plaza de Federico Moyúa; Ⓜ Moyúa

Length 2km; two hours

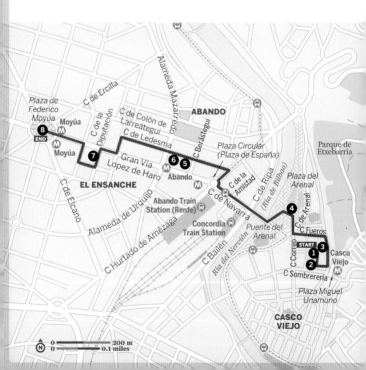

❶ Plaza Nueva

Plaza Nueva (Plaza Barria) is awash with *pintxo* bars, children racing around and adults socialising over a drink and a tasty titbit. On Sunday mornings a flea market takes place – rummage through old records, books, postcards, crockery and all manner of assorted odds and ends.

❷ Café-Bar Bilbao

Start your exploration of the square's culinary skills at the **Café-Bar Bilbao** (www.bilbao-cafe bar.com; Plaza Nueva 6; pintxos €2.50-3.50; ⏰7am-11pm Mon-Fri, 8.30am-10.30pm Sat, 10.30am-3pm Sun), with its cool blue southern Spanish tiles, warm northern atmosphere and superb array of *pintxos*.

❸ Sorginzulo

The **Sorginzulo** (Plaza Nueva 12; pintxos €2-3.50; ⏰7.30am-12.30am) is a matchbox-sized place with an exemplary spread. The house special of fried calamari is only served on weekends; other standouts include *bacalao al pil-pil* (cod in a garlicky sauce).

❹ Plaza del Arenal

The morphing ground between the Casco Viejo and the newer parts of Bilbao, Plaza del Arenal is a large open space that frequently plays host to outdoor exhibitions and on Sunday mornings is home to a fragrant flower market.

❺ Taberna Taurino

On one of central Bilbao's liveliest eating strips, **Taberna Taurino** (📞946 00 90 71; Calle Ledesma 5; pintxos €2-4; ⏰8am-1am Mon-Thu, to 2am Fri & Sat, 10am-3pm Sun; 🖋) has a striking interior of soaring latticed woodwork and glowing red lamps that complements Asian-accented *pintxo* hits, such as duck in crispy rice paper.

❻ Ledesma No 5

Everyone's favourite *pintxo* spot on restaurant-lined Ledesma, **Ledesma No 5** (Calle de Ledesma 5; pintxos €3-5.50; ⏰10am-11.30pm Mon-Wed, to 1am Thu, to 2.30am Fri, noon-2.30am Sat, to 11pm Sun) has phenomenal *pintxos* and small plates made from high-quality ingredients.

❼ El Globo

Congenial **El Globo** (www.bar elglobo.es; Calle de la Diputación 8; pintxos €2.50-4.50; ⏰8am-11pm Mon-Thu, to midnight Fri, 11am-midnight Sat) packs a fabulous range of creative small bites such as *txangurro gratinadao* (spider crab).

❽ Plaza de Federico Moyúa

With its fountains and spinning traffic, **Plaza de Federico Moyúa** (Plaza Mayor) is home to the regal Hotel Carlton, whose guests have included Einstein and Hemingway. Finish with a drink at its opulent interior bar or plaza-facing terrace.

Bilbao Old Town (Casco Viejo)

For reviews see

⊙	Sights	p37
✕	Eating	p39
🍷	Drinking	p43
★	Entertainment	p43
🔒	Shopping	p43

Puente del Ayuntamiento

Plaza Venezuela

C de Sendeja

Parque de Etxebarria

C de Ledesma

Gran Via Lopez de Haro

Plaza Circular (Plaza de España)

C de Ripa

C Villarías

C de la Amistad

Paseo del Arenal

C de Iparragirre

Ⓜ Abando

Abando

ABANDO

C de Navarra

Puente del Arenal

13 ✕

Plaza del Arenal

Iglesia San Nicolás de Bari

⊙ 3

Plaza de San Nicolás

C Hurtado de Amézaga

Ⓐ Abando Train Station (Renfe)

Ⓐ Concordia Train Station

Ría del Nervión (Ría de Bilbao)

Plaza Arriaga

C de Arenal

20 ★

C Fueros

Arriaga

16 ✕

C Ballén

C de la Ribera

CASCO VIEJO

C de Bidebarrieta

Plaza Nueva

8 ✕

7 ✕
11 ✕

Arkeologi Museo

⊙ 5

C de Santa María

14

22 ✕

24 🔒

25 🔒

Ⓜ Casco Viejo

9 ✕

21 ✕

C Jardines

C del Victor

C Correo

C Sombrerería

Plaza Miguel Unamuno

Euskal Museoa

⊙ 1

C de Iturribide

15 ✕

C del Perro

6 ⊙ Fuente del Perro

C Lotería

C de María Muñoz

C Hernani

M de La Merced

17

27 🔒

12 ✕

28 ✕

10 ✕

C Cintur

23 🔒

26 🔒

29 🔒

C Torre

C de la Pelota

C Barrenkale Barrenkale

4 ⊙

Catedral de Santiago

C Barrenkale

19

C Belostikale

C Carnicería Vieja

C Tendería

C de Artekale

30 ✕

C de Somera

C Ronda

18

Puente de la Ribera

Ribera

2 ✕ Las Siete Calles

Muelle Marzana

C de la Ribera

Mercado de la Ribera

N ⊙

0 — 200 m

0 — 0.1 miles

A   B   C   D

Sights

Euskal Museoa MUSEUM

1 ⊙ MAP P36, D4

One of Spain's best museums devoted to Basque culture takes visitors on a journey from Palaeolithic days to the 21st century, giving an overview of life among the boat builders, mariners, shepherds and artists who have left their mark on modern Basque identity. Displays of clothing, looms, fishing nets, model boats, woodcutters' axes, sheep bells and navigational instruments illustrate everyday life, while iconic round funerary stones help segue into topics of Basque rituals and beliefs. Parts of the museum closed for major renovations in late 2021. (Museo Vasco;

☑ 944 15 54 23; www.euskal-museoa. eus; Plaza Miguel Unamuno 4; adult/child €3/free, Thu free; ⊗10am-7pm Mon & Wed-Fri, 10am-1.30pm & 4-7pm Sat, 10am-2pm Sun)

Las Siete Calles AREA

2 ⊙ MAP P58, H6

Forming the heart of Bilbao's Casco Viejo are seven streets known as the Siete Calles (Zazpi Kaleak in Basque). These dark, atmospheric lanes – Barrenkale Barrena, Barrenkale, Carnicería Vieja, Belostikale, Tendería, Artekale and Somera – date to the 1400s, when the east bank of the Ría del Nervión (Ría de Bilbao) was first developed. They originally constituted the city's commercial centre and river port; these days

Bilbao Old Town (Casco Viejo) Sights

Mercado de la Ribera (p46) and Bilbao's Casco Vieja

CEBALLOS/SHUTTERSTOCK ©

they teem with lively cafes, *pintxo* bars and boutiques.

Iglesia San Nicolás de Bari

CHURCH

3 MAP P36, C3

This landmark church by the northern entrance to the Casco Viejo was consecrated in 1756. Dedicated to St Nicholas of Bari, the patron saint of sailors, it features a quadrangular baroque facade emblazoned with impressive heraldic stonework over the main portal, and two bell towers. (Plaza de San Nicolás; ⊙10.30am-1pm & 5.30-7.30pm Mon-Sat)

Catedral de Santiago

CATHEDRAL

4 MAP P36, C5

Towering above all in the Casco Viejo (although strangely invisible in the narrow streets) is the Catedral de Santiago, which has a vaulted cloister and Gothic Revival facade. Bilbao's oldest church, the cathedral dates back to the 14th century, though the Renaissance portico was added in 1571, following a fire. Above the main entrance, you'll spot scallop shells – symbols of Santiago (St James) and a reference for pilgrims on the northern route of the Camino de Santiago. (www.catedralbilbao.com; Plaza de Santiago; adult/child €5/free; ⊙10am-9pm Jul & Aug, to 8pm Sep-Jun)

Arkeologi Museo

MUSEUM

5 MAP P36, D4

This two-storey museum takes you deep into the past, beginning with 430,000-year-old fossils found in the Sierra de Atapuerca. On the 2nd floor, along the romp through the ages, you'll see models of early fortified villages, Celtiberian carvings, and statues and fragments

Four-headed Cross

The most visible symbol of Basque culture is the lauburu, or Basque cross. You'll see dozens of beautiful old examples of them inside the Euskal Museoa (p37) in Bilbao. 'Lauburu' means 'four heads' in Basque and it's so named because of the four comma-like heads. The meaning of this symbol is lost in the misty past – some say it represents the four old regions of the Basque country, others that it represents spirit, life, consciousness and form – but today many regard it as a symbol of prosperity. It's also used to signify life and death, and so is found on old headstones. Another theory as to its meaning is that it originally started appearing on 16th-century tombstones to indicate the grave of a healer of animals and souls (similar to a spiritual healer). When all is said and done, however, there's no real proof for any of these arguments.

from the Roman period; descend into the Visigothic times and the ensuing Middle Ages. Stones for catapults, a 10th-century tre-phined skull and jewellery from the 1200s are other curiosities. (Plaza Miguel Unamuno; adult/child €3.50/free, Fri free; ⏰10am-2pm & 4-7.30pm Tue-Sat)

Fuente del Perro FOUNTAIN

 6 MAP P36, C4

Designed by Juan Bautista de Oureta and Miguel de Maruri in 1800, this neoclassical fountain is located at a natural spring where market animals used to drink. Its three taps protrude from lion heads that more closely resemble their namesake *perro* (dog) heads. Spring water still flows here; bring a bottle to fill up. (Calle del Perro)

Eating

Casa Victor Montes BASQUE €€€

7 MAP P36, D4

The 1849-built Victor Montes attracts numerous luminaries but locals also appreciate its exquisite gilding, marble and frescoes, 1000-strong wine list and superb food. *Pintxos* span foie gras with cider jelly to *lomo* (cured pork sausage) with prawns and rum-soaked raisins. If you're planning a full meal, book in advance and savour the house special, *txuleta* (seven-year-old dairy cow T-bone

steak for two; €48). (☎944 15 70 67; www.victormontes.com; Plaza Nueva 8; mains €19.50-27.50, pintxos €2.80-6; ⏰1-4.45pm & 5-11pm)

Gure-Toki PINTXOS €

8 MAP P36, D3

One of the best *pintxo* bars in the Casco Viejo, this popular place serves creative and outstandingly good bites, including tender mini steak burgers, crispy croquettes, *bacalao al pil-pil* and various other delicacies adorned with edible flowers. (www.guretoki.com; Plaza Nueva 12; pintxos €3-5.50; ⏰9am-11.30pm Mon-Sat, 9.30am-4pm Sun)

Irrintzi PINTXOS €

9 MAP P36, B4

Just off the beaten path on Casco Viejo's western side, Irrintzi is a cosy, low-ceilinged eating and drinking spot, where a mostly local crowd files in for inventive bites not found elsewhere. Feast on tasty morsels such as white tuna with green-pepper salsa, crab and lemon croquettes, and tomato, pear and foie gras shots. Live music often plays on weekends. (www.irrintzi.es; Calle de Santa María 8; pintxos €2-4; ⏰9.30am-11pm Mon-Thu, 9.30am-midnight Fri, 11am-midnight Sat, noon-10pm Sun)

Baster PINTXOS €

10 MAP P36, C5

Relaxed Baster serves a range of outstanding *pintxos*, including

Basque Language

The Basque language, known as Euskara, is the oldest in Europe and has no known connection to any Indo-European languages. Suppressed by Franco, Basque was subsequently recognised as one of Spain's official languages, with 751,500 speakers in total (a 6% growth rate in the past 25 years), of which 93% of speakers are on the Spanish side and 6.8% are on the French side (nearly all speakers are bilingual). It has become the language of choice among a growing number of young Basques in particular (55.4% of 16- to 24-year-olds speak it).

While visiting, you'll find that speaking at least a few words of Basque is greatly appreciated by locals. See the language chapter p167 for more info.

octopus skewers with potato, mini-quiches, house-made croquettes and delectable *jamón* (ham). Pair them with a glass of refreshing *txakoli* (local white wine) or vermouth, or choose from its extensive range of local craft beers. It gets very busy at weekend lunchtimes, when bar-hoppers crowd its pavement tables and bright, modern interior. (www.facebook.com/basterbilbao; Calle Correo 22; pintxos €2-4; ⏰9.30am-10pm Tue-Thu, to 11pm Fri & Sat, to 4pm Sun; 🛜)

Bar Charly

PINTXOS €

11 🍴 MAP P36, D4

In an unrivalled location on Plaza Nueva, Bar Charly lays out *pintxos* for garrulous afternoon and evening crowds. There are at least three vegetarian *pintxos* per day, such as a roast courgette and mushroom *montadito* (mini baguette), or spinach and goat's-cheese croquettes; other dishes might include smoked salmon and anchovies with black caviar or crab mayonnaise. (www.barcharly.com; Plaza Nueva 8; pintxos €2.50-6; ⏰10am-10pm Sun-Thu, to 11.30pm Fri & Sat; 🖊)

Rio-Oja

BASQUE €€

12 🍴 MAP P36, B4

Going strong since 1959, Rio-Oja retains a rock-solid reputation for its traditional Basque dishes. Its *cazuelitas* (stews served in the clay ramekins in which they're cooked) are ideal for sharing – varieties include *cordero guisado* (braised lamb) and *chipirones en sur tinta* (squid cooked in its own ink), as well as inland specialities such as snails, tripe and sheep brains. (📞944 15 08 71; www.rio-oja.com; Calle del Perro 4; mains €16-26; ⏰9am-11pm Tue-Sun)

Claudio: La Feria del Jamón

PINTXOS €

13 🍴 MAP P36, C2

A creaky old place full of ancient furnishings, Claudio has scarcely changed since it opened in 1948. As you'll guess from the name and the hams hanging from the ceiling, it's all about pigs, including *lomo* (air-dried pork loin), *morcilla* (blood sausage), chorizo, and *salchichón* (smoked sausage), accompanied by local cheeses and wines. Opposite the bar is a shop selling hams. (www.claudiojamones. com; Calle de Iparragirre 9-11; pintxos €2.80-5; ⌚5.30-11pm Mon-Thu, 5.30-11.30pm Fri, 6-11.30pm Sat)

Berton

PINTXOS €

14 MAP P36, B4

Tucked in a narrow lane, rustic Berton lures you in with a long wooden bar topped with tiny delicacies and frothy pilsner on tap. Glistening slices of *jamón*, deep-fried Gernika chillies, mushrooms stuffed with garlic and sheep's cheese, blood sausage with red pepper, and spider crab in squid ink are all served in an exposed brick, stone and timber setting. (www.berton. eus; Calle Jardines 11; pintxos €2-4.50; ⌚8.30am-midnight Wed-Mon; 🛜)

El Txoko Berria

BASQUE €€

15 MAP P36, B4

Set over two levels, with a beautifully tiled ground floor dining room and a more contemporary space above, this welcoming restaurant excels at staples such as pork cheeks cooked in La Rioja red wine, cod *Bizkaina* style (with a sweet, slightly spicy pepper sauce) and risotto with mushrooms and smoked Idiazabal sheep's cheese. (📞944 79 42 98; www.eltxokoberria. com; Calle de Bidebarrieta 14; mains €8-16.50; ⌚1-4pm & 7.30-11pm Sun-Thu, to midnight Fri & Sat)

Teatro Arriaga (p43)

JON CHICA/SHUTTERSTOCK ©

Los Fueros

BASQUE €€

16 ⊗ MAP P36, C3

Seafood stars at this backstreet bar-restaurant near Plaza Nueva, appearing in dishes such as cider-marinated sardines, chargrilled octopus, mussels steamed in *txakoli* (white wine) and dorado with salsa verde. Extending to a mezzanine, the rustic-contemporary setting is more stylish than many old town places, decked out in off-white and jade-green mosaic tiling and gleaming timber tables. (☐944 15

The Art of Eating Pintxos

Just rolling the word *pintxo* ('peen-cho') around your tongue defines the essence of this cheerful, cheeky little slice of Basque cuisine. The perfect *pintxo* should have exquisite taste, texture and appearance, and should be savoured in two elegant bites. The Basque version of a tapa, the *pintxo* transcends the commonplace with its culinary panache.

Many *pintxos* are bedded on small pieces of bread or on tiny half-baguettes, upon which towering creations are constructed. Some bars specialise in seafood, with much use of marinated anchovies, prawns and strips of squid, all topped with anything from shredded crab to pâté. Others deal in pepper or mushroom delicacies, or simply offer a mix of everything. And the choice isn't normally limited to what's on the bar top in front of you: many of the best *pintxos* are the hot ones you need to order.

For many visitors, ordering *pintxos* can seem like one of the dark arts of local etiquette. Fear not: in many bars in Bilbao, San Sebastián and the Basque Country, it couldn't be easier. With so many *pintxo* varieties lined up along the bar, you either take a small plate and help yourself or point to the morsel you want. Otherwise, many places have a list of *pintxos*, either on a menu or posted up behind the bar. If you can't choose, ask for 'la especialidad de la casa' (the house speciality) and it's hard to go wrong.

Another way of eating *pintxos* is to order *raciones* (literally 'rations'; large *pintxo* servings) or *medias raciones* (half-rations; bigger plates than tapas servings but smaller than standard *raciones*). These plates and half-plates of a particular dish are a good way to go if you particularly like something and want more than a mere *pintxo*. After a couple of *raciones*, however, most people are full.

Locals often prefer to just have one or two *pintxos* in each bar before moving on to the next place. Bear in mind that *pintxos* are never free. In fact, the cost of a few mouthfuls can quickly add up.

30 47; www.losfueros.com; Calle Fueros 6; pintxos €5-6.50, mains €12-24; ⏲12.30-4pm & 8-11pm Mon & Wed-Sat, noon-3.30pm & 8-11pm Sun)

Drinking

La Peña Athletic

BAR

17 MAP P36, B5

A must for all fans of Bilbao's famed football team, La Peña Athletic is covered with vintage jerseys, trophies, old team photos and oil paintings of legendary past players. It pulls a mix of old-timers and young enthusiasts, who come to raise a glass (and snack on *pintxos*) to the boys in red and white while watching a game. (www.restauranteathletic.es; Calle de la Pelota 5; ⏲1-4pm & 8-11.30pm)

Bohemian Lane

CAFE

18 MAP P36, B5

Inviting coffeehouse Bohemian Lane has wicker chairs, furniture made from salvaged wooden pallets and mismatched cushions. A laid-back spot for Fair Trade coffee and tea, and organic fresh juices, it also whips up tartines (open-faced sandwiches), cinnamon rolls, cookies and other sweets that are 100% vegan. (www.bohemianlane bilbao.com; Calle Carnicería Vieja 3; ⏲10am-8.30pm Mon-Sat, 3.30-8.30pm Sun)

Hells Bells

BAR

19 MAP P36, B5

Plastered with posters, guitars and other memorabilia, dimly lit Hells Bells blasts out tracks from bands such as AC/DC, Judas Priest, Mötley Crüe, Kiss and Metallica, accompanied by cheap beer. If there's a rock or metal concert in Bilbao, you can be sure the after-party will be held here. (Calle Barrenkale 8; ⏲8pm-2.30am Thu, to 4am Fri & Sat)

Entertainment

Teatro Arriaga

THEATRE

20 MAP P36, B3

The neobaroque facade of this 1200-seat venue commands the open spaces of El Arenal between the Casco Viejo and the river. It stages theatrical performances and classical music concerts. Guided behind-the-scenes tours lasting 50 minutes in English, Spanish and Basque (adult/child €5/free) take place hourly from 11am to 1pm on Saturdays and Sundays. (☏944 79 20 36; www.teatroarriaga.eus; Plaza Arriaga)

Shopping

Ätakontu

FASHION & ACCESSORIES

21 MAP P36, B4

A pair of Bilbao textile artists created this small shop, which is making waves across the Basque Country. Graphic T-shirts are the

Basque Festivals & Events

The Basques love a good festival. Every town, city and most villages have their own week of mayhem, and during the summer you'll almost certainly come across a celebration on your travels. Highlights include:

Aste Nagusia (☺ mid-Aug) Held over nine days, Bilbao's grandest fiesta begins on the first Saturday after 15 August. Its full program of cultural events features music and dancing, Basque rural sports (such as chopping wood and lifting heavy stones), parades of giants and fireworks.

Bay of Biscay Festival (www.bayofbiscayfestival.eus; ☺ late Jul) In the Central Basque Coast town of Bermeo, this three-day festival combines indie, rock and alternate concerts by Basque and Spanish bands with a celebration of the area's culinary scene, from Michelin-starred food trucks to cookery demonstrations and workshops.

Bilbao BBK Live (www.bilbaobbklive.com; ☺ Jul) Bilbao's biggest musical event draws top artists from around the globe. It takes place over three days (typically early to mid-July) in Parque Kobetamendi, a hillside park located 3km west of the centre.

Carnaval (☺ Feb or Mar) Both Bilbao and San Sebastián celebrate over six days, from the Thursday before Ash Wednesday to Shrove Tuesday.

Getxo Jazz (www.getxo.eus; ☺ late Jun-early Jul) The line-up at Getxo's jazz festival is usually impressive, featuring international stars on the main stage at Plaza Biotz Alai, along with free concerts by up-and-coming musicians on Plaza Estación de Algorta.

Dia de San Sebastián (☺ 19-20 Jan) San Sebastián celebrates its patron saint with fervour. The big event is the Tamborrada, when thousands of drummers wearing 19th-century military dress and chefs' whites parade through the city.

San Sebastián International Film Festival (www.sansebastianfestival. com; ☺ Sep) The world-renowned film festival usually features an excellent line-up of films from Europe, the US and Latin America, with a few big premieres. Screenings take place at venues citywide.

Semana Grande (http://astenagusia.donostiakultura.eus; ☺ mid-Aug) Known as Aste Nagusia in Basque, San Sebastián's big summer festival features an action-packed line-up of street parties, concerts and nightly fireworks competitions, plus rural sports, children's activities, and parades with giants and oversized heads.

speciality, featuring whimsical and art-naïf designs; all are manufactured locally, made with organic cotton and come in unisex sizes. And with limited production runs, you won't see these elsewhere. (www.atakontu.es; Calle Jardines 8; ⏰11am-2.30pm & 5-8pm Mon-Sat)

La Quesaría
FOOD & DRINKS

22 🅐 MAP P36, B4

Cheese lovers shouldn't miss this wondrous shop. You'll find more than 40 varieties of the good stuff, with new selections every week. It's also worth browsing the selection of microbrews (try a pale ale from the Bidassoa Basque Brewery), wines, local jams and other goodies. (www.facebook.com/

laqueseriabilbao; Calle Jardines 10; ⏰10.30am-2pm & 5-8.30pm Mon-Sat, 11am-3pm Sun)

Peletería Ramón Ezkerra
FASHION

23 🅐 MAP P36, C5

At Bilbao-born Ramón Ezkerra's atelier, limited-edition pieces handcrafted from sustainably sourced Basque and Spanish leather are primarily made on site. Along with stylish jackets for men and women, you'll find bags, hats, gloves, leather dresses, jumpsuits and trousers. Clothing can be tailored to fit. (www.ramonezkerra. com; Calle Correo 23; ⏰10am-1.30pm & 4.30-8pm Mon-Sat)

Semana Grande celebrations, Bilbao

Mercado de la Ribera

Overlooking the river, the **Mercado de la Ribera** (Map p36, C6; www.mercadodelaribera. biz; Calle de la Ribera; ⏰8am-2.30pm Mon & Sat, 8am-2.30pm & 5-8pm Tue-Fri) is an expansive food market that draws many of the city's top chefs for their morning selection of fresh produce. If you're not planning a picnic, don't miss the *pintxo* counters upstairs (open till 10pm), which offer an excellent spread – plus seating indoors and out.

Gorostiga   HATS

24 🔒 MAP P36, C4

Gorostiga has been crafting traditional *txapelas* (Basque berets) and hats since 1857. Its nine different berets cover all parts of the Basque Country, including the flat-topped berets worn in Bilbao, the tilted style of the French Basque Country, and the oversized *txapeldun* typically worn at festivals, weddings and other celebrations. (www.facebook.com/sombrerosgorostiaga; Calle del Victor 9; ⏰10am-1.30pm & 4-8pm Mon-Fri, 10am-1.30pm Sat)

Le Chocolat   CHOCOLATE

25 🔒 MAP P36, D4

The Bilbao-inspired treats here include chocolates in the shape of pavement tiles and Athletic Bilbao football jerseys. At Christmas, it's also one of the best places for seasonal local speciality *sokonusko* – layered nougat based on a Mayan recipe brought back to the city by Bilbao adventurer Iñigo Urrutia, who travelled to Mexico in 1881 in search of El Dorado. (www.lechocolat.es; Calle Sombrerería 11; ⏰10.30am-2pm & 5-8pm Mon-Sat)

Rzik   FASHION & ACCESSORIES

26 🔒 MAP P36, C5

Street fashion goes green at this hip little store, where everything is made from recycled materials. You'll find colourful messenger bags made from old advertising banners, sleek backpacks made of truck tyres and eye-catching belts made from former firefighter hoses. The designs are bright and bold – and make fine conversation pieces. (www.rzik.es; Calle Correo 25; ⏰11am-2.30pm & 5-8.30pm Mon-Sat)

Hasiberriro   VINTAGE

27 🔒 MAP P36, B5

You'll find some excellent deals at this secondhand clothing and book store tucked into the Casco Viejo. There's apparel for both men and women here, including dresses, skirts and accessories. It's run by an NGO, with profits supporting various social projects. (www.facebook.com/hasiberriro; Calle Barrenkale Barrena 9; ⏰10am-8pm Mon-Fri, 11am-2pm Sat)

La Bendita
FOOD & DRINKS

28 MAP P36, C4

The gourmet delicacies at La Bendita are sourced almost exclusively from the Basque Country. You'll find chocolates, foie gras, anchovies, olive oils, pâté, and drinks including *patxaran* (a sloe-berry liqueur) and *txakoli* (local white wine). (www.la benditabilbao.com; Calle de Bidebarrieta 16; 4.30-8.30pm Mon, 10.30am-2pm & 4.30-8.30pm Tue-Sat, noon-2pm Sun)

Orriak
ARTS & CRAFTS

29 MAP P36, C5

Easy to miss, this delightful little shop is a great spot when browsing for gifts, most of which are made in store or elsewhere in the Basque Country. Whether it's jewellery, mugs and other homewares, most products come emblazoned with Basque symbols. (www.orriak. com; Calle de Artekale 54; 4.30-8pm Mon, 10am-1.30pm & 4.30-8pm Tue-Sat)

Almacen Coloniales y Bacalao Gregorio Martín
FOOD

30 MAP P36, C5

Specialising in *bacalao* (salted cod) from the Faroe Islands since 1931, this iconic boutique also sells oils, cheese, wine, beans and pulses, and hams and other charcuterie. (www.gregoriomartin.es; Calle de Artekale 22; 9am-1.15pm & 4.30-7.45pm Mon-Fri, 9am-1.30pm Sat)

Almacen Coloniales y Bacalao Gregorio Martín

Explore ⊛

Bilbao New Town

Bilbao's elegant new town has an impressive spread of attractions. The neighbourhood is home to world-class and fascinating under-the-radar museums, beautiful river views and walks, and some of the best restaurants and bars in the region.

The Short List

○ **Museo Guggenheim Bilbao (p50)** *Exploring the iconic vantage points and hidden facets of this astonishing architectural wonder.*

○ **Museo de Bellas Artes (p54)** *Wandering through galleries lined with sculptures and paintings by renowned artists from the Basque Country and beyond.*

○ **Estadio San Mamés (p67)** *Joining thousands of frenzied fans as they cheer on Athletic Bilbao.*

○ **Azkuna Zentroa (p60)** *Checking out contemporary art or catching an indie film inside the imaginative Alhóndiga cultural centre.*

○ **Funicular de Artxanda (p61)** *Riding to the top of Artxanda for mesmerising city views.*

Getting There & Around

Ⓜ Useful metro stations include Moyúa, bang in the heart of town; Abando for shopping; and San Mamés for the bus station.

🚃 The tram runs along the length of the river with a stop close to the Museo Guggenheim Bilbao.

🚶 It's a five-minute walk from the Museo Guggenheim Bilbao to the city centre.

Neighbourhood Map on p58

Athletic Bilbao playing at Estadio San Mamés (p67)

Top Experience 📷
Explore the Iconic Museo Guggenheim Bilbao

Opened in 1997, Bilbao's shimmering museum is one of modern architecture's most iconic buildings. The museum almost single-handedly lifted Bilbao out of its postindustrial depression and into the 21st century, stimulating further development and placing Bilbao firmly in the spotlight. For many travellers, this extraordinary building is the primary reason for visiting Bilbao.

◎ MAP P58, E1

✆ 944 35 90 80

www.guggenheim-bilbao.eus

Avenida Abandoibarra 2

adult/child €13/free

🕙 10am-8pm, closed Mon Sep-Jun

The Design

For most visitors, it's the architecture itself that is the real star of the Guggenheim show. Designed by Canadian-born American architect Frank Gehry, the museum's flowing canopies, promontories, ship-like shapes, towers and flying fins, all covered in gleaming titanium tiles, are irresistible. Allow plenty of time to walk around the building's exterior, observing how the patterns and colours change with the light.

Puppy

Outside, on the city side of the museum, is Jeff Koons' kitsch whimsy *Puppy,* a 12m-tall Highland terrier made up of thousands of flowers. Originally a temporary exhibition, Bilbao has hung on to 'El Poop'. *Bilbaínos* will tell you that El Poop came first – and then they built a kennel behind it.

Tall Tree & the Eye

An exterior highlight is Anish Kapoor's work, *Tall Tree & the Eye*. It consists of 73 reflective spheres anchored around three axes, each of which distorts reality as you look into it.

Fog Sculpture #08025 (FOG)

Lying between the glass buttresses of the central atrium and Ría del Nervión (Ría de Bilbao) outside the museum is this installation by Fujiko Nakaya: a simple pool of water that regularly emits a mist. In case you missed the play on words here, FOG are also the initials of the building's architect.

Fire Fountain

On the northern side of the museum opposite the river is Yves Klein's *Fire Fountain,* conceived by the artist but only realised here after his

★ Top Tips

● The Artean Pass (adult €17) is a joint ticket for the Museo de Bellas Artes (p54) and the Museo Guggenheim Bilbao, offering significant savings. It's available at both museums.

● Entry queues can be huge in busy times; you're best prebooking online with an allocated time slot.

● For a bird's-eye perspective of the museum, ride the Funicular de Artxanda (p61) to the park high above the city.

✕ Take a Break

The Guggenheim's Nerua (p63) restaurant serves refined Basque cuisine.

Cheaper and less formal is the **Bistró Guggenheim Bilbao** (☏944 23 93 33; www.bistroguggen heimbilbao.com; 2-/3-course menu €22/30; ⏱1-3pm & 8-10.30pm Jul & Aug, 1-3pm Tue-Sun & 8-10.30pm Thu-Sat Sep-Jun).

death. At night, its five jets of fire dance above a water-filled pool and illuminate the building's walls.

Maman

On the riverbank just outside the museum is Louise Bourgeois' sculpture *Maman*: a skeletal, spider-like canopy said to symbolise a protective embrace.

Atrium

The atrium, a huge cathedral-like space, serves as your first taste of the museum's interior. Light pours into this entrance gallery through what appear to be glass cliffs. At one end, Jenny Holzer's nine LED columns of ever-flowing phrases and text fragments (in English, Spanish and Basque) appear to reach for the skies. The space was designed to provide views of the river and surrounding hills.

Tulips

From the atrium head out onto the little terrace surrounded by shallow pools of water to see Jeff Koons' stainless steel *Tulips*, whose bubbly, colourful form in Christmas bauble–style high gloss represents a bouquet of giant balloon flowers (more than 2m tall and 5m across). The work belongs to his ambitious *Celebration* series.

The Matter of Time

The ground floor of the museum is devoted to permanent exhibitions. One of the most popular with visitors is Richard Serra's rust-red

Tulips by Jeff Koons

The Vision Behind the Masterpiece

Designed by celebrated architect Frank Gehry, the Museo Guggenheim Bilbao dominates the city's waterfront, its look and mood changing with the rising and falling light. The building sits on a former industrial wasteland and the city's shipping, industrial and fishing heritage is evoked in its form, which some describe as resembling a ship or a shimmering fish.

After the collapse of shipping and heavy industry in Bilbao, the authorities embarked on a regeneration of the city. One of the key requirements was a world-class cultural exhibition space, and from that idea came the Museo Guggenheim Bilbao.

Since its opening in 1997, the museum has done much to transform Bilbao from run-down industrial city to bona fide cultural hub. As well as playing off the city's historical and geographical context, the building reflects Gehry's own interests, not least his engagement with industrial materials. The titanium tiles that sheathe most of the building like giant scales are said to have been inspired by the architect's childhood fascination with fish.

The Matter of Time. Despite the grand name, this is best described as a giant steel maze that visitors are free to wander through, which often seems to serve as much as a children's playground as a work of art.

In the room's northeastern corner is a small exhibition on the work's conceptualisation, fabrication and installation, including a scale model.

Lightning with Stag in its Glare

Created by German artist Joseph Beuys, this installation's suspended bronze triangle represents a bolt of lightning illuminating various startled animals. The three-wheeled cart represents a goat and the upended ironing board a stag. It's Beuys' only metallic work.

How Profound is the Air

The work of San Sebastián native Eduardo Chillida, who studied architecture in Madrid before taking up art, permanent exhibit *How Profound Is The Air* is sculpted from alabaster, juxtaposing a rough natural-stone exterior and highly polished interior.

Temporary Exhibitions

The museum's exceptional temporary shows – from retrospectives of the groundbreaking contemporary video artist Bill Viola to wide-ranging exhibitions that explore *fin de siècle* Paris – are the main attraction for many visitors.

Top Experience 📷
Admire Fine Art at Museo de Bellas Artes

Bilbao's fine arts museum might not have the glitz and glamour of the nearby Museo Guggenheim Bilbao, but the exhibits here more than hold their own. Collections range from works by well-known masters such as Goya and El Greco to pieces by more modern artists. Equally renowned are its temporary exhibitions.

◎ MAP P58, D3

📞 944 39 60 60

www.museobilbao.com

Plaza del Museo 2

adult/child €10/free, 6-8pm free

🕐 10am-8pm Wed-Mon

Classical Collection

The heart of the museum's huge collection of art (some 10,000 pieces) consists of the classical collection, with works dating from the 12th to 19th centuries. Showstoppers include Murillo's *St Peter in Tears,* which depicts St Peter at the moment of his repentance. El Greco's *The Annunciation* also draws crowds, as does Goya's *Portrait of Martín Zapater*.

Contemporary Collection

Stars of the contemporary collection, which covers the period from the 20th century onwards, include Paul Gauguin's *Laveuses à Arles,* depicting washerwomen in Arles, France, where Gauguin lived for a time. Also look out for Francis Bacon's *Lying Figure in a Mirror,* which shows, in a rather abstract way, a male figure reflected in a mirror.

Basque Collection

The Basque Country's finest art gallery wouldn't be complete without a comprehensive body of work from the region's best-known artists. This includes sculptor Eduardo Chillida's *Trembling Irons II,* one of the pieces that brought him to worldwide attention. Ignacio Zuloaga and Juan de Echevarría are also represented.

Temporary Exhibitions

The permanent collection of the Museo de Bellas Artes is one of the finest in Spain outside of Madrid, but the temporary exhibitions are what really draw the crowds. See the website for details of upcoming exhibitions.

★ Top Tips

o Take advantage of free entry between 6pm and 8pm.

o Save money with the Artean Pass (€17), covering the Museo de Bellas Artes and the Museo Guggenheim Bilbao.

o Queues for temporary exhibitions can be very long. Buy an advance ticket online.

o Learn more by picking up an audio guide (included in adult admission, €3 for children) at the museum entrance.

✕ Take a Break

Enjoy *pintxos,* sandwiches and drinks at the museum's on-site cafe, which has lovely outdoor seating surrounded by trees.

Nearby **Colombo** (🖉 944 39 22 45; www.colombobilbao.com; Calle de Rodríguez Arias 32; mains €10-19; 🕑 1-4pm & 8-11pm Sun-Thu, to 11.30pm Fri & Sat; 🖉) serves globally inspired cuisine in an atmospheric vintage-style setting.

Walking Tour 🥾

Architecture & River Views

Bilbao rewards those who take the time to walk its streets admiring the contrasting collections of architectural styles, enjoying the riverside walkways and passing plenty of places where you can sample a drink and pintxo or two. This walk takes you past the most memorable historic and contemporary buildings in the city.

Walk Facts

Start/Finish Concordia train station; M Abando

Length 6km; three hours

❶ Concordia Train Station

Start at one of the city's architectural treasures, the 1902-built **Concordia train station** (Estación de Santander; Calle Lopez de Haro), with its beautifully tiled art nouveau facade.

❷ Teatro Campos Elíseos

Another art nouveau beauty, the Teatro Campos Elíseos (p68), also dates from 1902. Since its restoration in 2010, it stages theatre and musical performances.

❸ Jardines Albia

The leafy Jardines Albia, overlooked by the 16th-century Iglesia San Vicente Mártir, are a peaceful spot to rest up, with a fountain at the gardens' centre.

❹ Museo de Bellas Artes

A 1945-built neoclassical building, added to in 1970 and again in 1996, houses Bilbao's splendid fine arts museum, the Museo de Bellas Artes (p54).

❺ Parque de Doña Casilda de Iturrizar

Stroll through the **Parque de Doña Casilda de Iturrizar** (p61) with its bandstands and duck ponds.

❻ Itsasmuseum

To get a sense of Bilbao's industrial past, stop outside the city's maritime museum, the Itsasmuseum (p60). On the museum's western side, opposite the dry docks, you'll see the bright-red 'Carola' crane (1957) formerly used for shipbuilding.

❼ Torre Iberdrola

Rising up (and up) from the river's southern bank, the obelisk-like Torre Iberdrola is a 165m-high, 41-storey glinting glass office block. Inaugurated in 2012, it's the tallest building in the region.

❽ Museo Guggenheim Bilbao

Head to the city's most famous building, the Museo Guggenheim Bilbao (p50) – a titanium masterpiece that changed perceptions of modern architecture when it opened in 1997. Outside the museum, check out iconic sculptures including Louise Bourgeois' spider-like *Maman* and Jeff Koons' flower-adorned *Puppy*.

❾ Puente Zubizuri

Continue upriver to the Puente Zubizuri (p61), the striking wave-like bridge designed in 1997 by Santiago Calatrava.

❿ Teatro Arriaga

Built in 1890, Bilbao's beautiful neobaroque Teatro Arriaga (p43) in the Casco Viejo is home to the city opera and hosts classical music. From here, cross the river over the Puente del Arenal to return to Concordia train station.

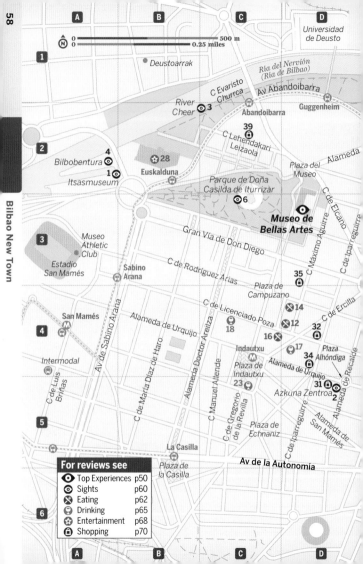

A **B** **C** **D**

Universidad de Deusto

0 — 500 m
0 — 0.25 miles

Deustoarrak

Rīa del Nervión
(Rīa de Bilbao)

C Evaristo Churrca

Av Abandoibarra

River Cheer ◉3

Abandoibarra

Guggenheim

C Lehendakari Leizaola
39

Bilbobentura ◉4

☆28 Euskalduna

1◉

Itsasmuseum

Plaza del Museo

Alameda

Parque de Doña Casilda de Iturrizar
◉6

Museo de
Bellas Artes ◉

Museo Athletic Club

Gran Vía de Don Diego

C de Rodríguez Arias

C Máximo Aguirre

C de Elcano

C de Iparraguirre

Estadio San Mamés

Sabino Arana

Plaza de Campuzano
35 ⊕

San Mamés Ⓜ

Alameda de Urquijo

C de Licenciado Poza
18 ⊕

⊗14

C de Ercilla

⊗12

32 ⊕

Intermodal

16⊗

Indautxu Ⓜ

17 ⊕

Plaza Alhóndiga
34 ⊕

C de Luis Briñas

C de María Díaz de Haro

Alameda Doctor Areitza

C Manuel Allende

Plaza de Indautxu

23 ⊕

Alameda de Urquijo

Azkuna Zentroa

31 ⊕◉2

Plaza de Recalde

Alameda de San Mamés

C de Gregorio de la Revilla

Plaza de Echaniz

C de Iparraguirre

La Casilla

Plaza de la Casilla

Av de la Autonomía

For reviews see

◉	Top Experiences	p50
◉	Sights	p60
⊗	Eating	p62
⊕	Drinking	p65
☆	Entertainment	p68
⊕	Shopping	p70

A **B** **C** **D**

E

F

G

H

Bilbao ✈ (11km)

Av de las Universidades

Museo Guggenheim Bilbao ◉

11 ✕

Mazarredo

Av Maurice Ravel

7 ◉ Funicular de Artxanda

C Castaños

C Huertas de la Villa

Paseo Campo Volantin

1

2

C Lersundi

19 15

C de Cosme Echevarrieta

22 ✕

C Barraincua

C de Recalde

C de Los Heros

Alameda Mazarredo

C de Ercilla

C de Henao

9 ✕

Uribitarte

Uribitarte

5 ◉ Zubizuri

25

C San Vincente

30

26

C Ibañez de Bilbao

13 Barroeta Aldamar

Pio Baroja

Plaza Venezuela

Puente del Ayuntamiento

Parque de Etxebarria

Av Zumalacárregui

3

Plaza de Jado

C de Colón de Larreátegui

Plaza del Ensanche

ABANDO

C Basquery

Plaza de Federico Moyúa Ⓜ Moyúa

Ⓜ Moyúa

C de la Diputación

36 Gran Via Lopez de Haro

8 ✕

C de Ledesma

C de Berasteguí

20

C Buenos Aires

21 37

33 Abando

C de Villaras

C de Ripa

C Príncipe

Plaza del Arenal

4

EL ENSANCHE

C de Elcano

C del General Concha

Alameda de Urquijo

C de Luxana

27

C Hurtado de Amézaga

10

Euskalduna

Abando Ⓜ

Abando Train Station (Renfe)

Plaza Circular (Plaza de España)

C de Navarra

Concordia Train Station

Puente del Arenal

Plaza Arriaga

C de Arenal

Plaza Nueva

Casco Ⓜ Viejo

5

Plaza de Zabalburu

Juan de Garay Kalea

C de García Salazar

24

C Bailén

C Lamana

38 29

C Hernani

M de la Merced

Rio del Nervión (Ria de Bilbao)

Arriaga

CASCO VIEJO

C de La Ribera

Las Siete Calles

◉ Ribera

6

E

F

G

H

Sights

Itsasmuseum
MUSEUM

1 ⦿ MAP P58, A2

On the waterfront, this interactive maritime museum brings the watery depths of Bilbao and Basque maritime history to life. Start with a 10-minute video for an overview of Bilbao history from the 1300s to the present before wandering through the two floors of displays, which show old shipbuilding techniques, harrowing shipwrecks (and innovative coastal rescue strategies), pirate threats and intricate models – including a full-scale recreation of the 1511 Consulate Barge. Outdoors, you can clamber about on a range of boats. (📞946 08 55 00; www.itsasmuseum.eus; Muelle Ramón de la Sota 1; adult/child €6/free, free Tue Sep-Jun; ⏰10am-8pm Tue-Sun Apr-Oct, to 6pm Tue-Fri, to 8pm Sat & Sun Nov-Mar; 👶)

Azkuna Zentroa
ARCHITECTURE

2 ⦿ MAP P58, D5

Take a neglected wine storage warehouse, convert it into a leisure and cultural centre, add a shot of Bilbao style and the result is the Azkuna Zentroa (Alhóndiga in Basque). Repurposed by renowned architect Philippe Starck, it now houses a cinema, art gallery, rooftop swimming pool with a glass bottom, a public media centre, cafes and restaurants. The ground floor is notable for its 43 tubby columns, each constructed with a unique design symbolising infinite cultures, architecture, wars and religion. (📞944 01 40 14; www.azkunazentroa.eus; Plaza Alhóndiga 4; ⏰7am-11pm Mon-Thu, to midnight Fri, 8.30am-midnight Sat, to 11pm Sun)

River Cheer
BOATING

3 ⦿ MAP P58, C2

River Cheer puts you at the helm of a small four-person canopy-shaded aluminium boat, which you can pilot along the Nervión as far upstream as the old town, via the Guggenheim, with fantastic photo opportunities, and downstream to Getxo. No license or experience is required; you're given a short tutorial before heading out. It's best to book in advance. (📞622 932 042; www.rivercheer.com; Calle Evaristo Churruca 1; boat hire per 2/4 hours €70/120)

Bilbobentura
WATER SPORTS

4 ⦿ MAP P58, A2

This dockside outfit hires out single and double kayaks and SUP boards. It also offers various group outings, including evening paddles (€20; 8.30pm Friday June to October). Life jackets and waterproof bags are included; lockers and changing rooms are available at the premises. (📞660 734 953; www.bilbobentura.com; Muelle Ramón de la Sota 1; kayak hire per 1/2/8hr from €10/14/45, SUP per 2/8hr €8/20; ⏰10am-8pm Apr-Oct)

Zubizuri

BRIDGE

5 🎯 MAP P58, G2

The most striking of the modern bridges that span the Ría del Nervión, the Zubizuri (Basque for 'White Bridge') has become an iconic feature of Bilbao's cityscape since its completion in 1997. The work of Spanish architect Santiago Calatrava, it has a curved glass-brick walkway (slippery when wet) suspended under a flowing white arch to which it's attached by a series of steel spokes.

Parque de Doña Casilda de Iturrizar

PARK

6 🎯 MAP P58, C3

Planted with maples, lindens, cedars, palms and 70 other species of trees, the Parque de Doña Casilda de Iturrizar was completed in 1920, and is a lovely spot to while away an afternoon. The centrepiece of this elegant, English-style park is the small pond filled with ducks and swans. (Paseo de José Anselmo Clavé)

Funicular de Artxanda

FUNICULAR

7 🎯 MAP P58, G1

Bilbao is a city hemmed in by hills and mountains, resting in a tight valley. For a breathtaking view over the city and the wild Basque mountains beyond, take a trip on the funicular railway that has creaked its way up the steep slope to the summit of Artxanda since 1915 – it's well worth the journey. (Plaza Funicular; adult/child one-way €2/0.31;

Zubizuri

SAIKO3P/SHUTTERSTOCK ©

Bilbao Background

Bilbao was granted the title of *villa* (city-state) in 1300 and medieval *bilbaínos* went about their business in the bustle of Las Siete Calles (p37), the original seven streets of the old town, and down on the wharves. The conquest of the Americas stimulated trade and Basque fishers, merchants and settlers soon built strong links to cities such as Boston. By the late 19th century, the smokestacks of steelworks, shipbuilding yards and chemical plants dominated the area's skyline.

From the Carlist Wars through to the Spanish Civil War, Bilbao was always considered the greatest prize in the north, largely for its industrial value. Franco took the city in the spring of 1937 and reprisals against Basque nationalists were massive and long lasting. Yet during the Franco era, the city prospered as it fed Spanish industrial needs. This was followed by the seemingly terminal economic decline that has been so dynamically reversed since the mid 1990s, as Bilbao has transitioned to a service-based economy and a tourist and cultural hotspot.

⏱ every 15min 7.15am-10pm Mon-Thu, to 11pm Fri & Sat, 8.15am-10pm Sun Jun-Sep, 7.15am-10pm Oct-May)

Eating

La Viña del Ensanche
PINTXOS €€

8 ⊗ MAP P58, E4

With old-fashioned wood-panelled walls and framed postcards written by adoring fans over the years, La Viña del Ensanche maintains a reputation as one of Bilbao's best eating spots – no small achievement for a place that has been in business since 1927. Mouthwatering morsels of ham, seared mackerel and crispy asparagus tempura are just a few of the many temptations. (📞944 15 56 15; www. lavinadelensanche.com; Calle de la Diputación 10; small plates €5-22.50, tasting menu €35; ⏱8.30am-11pm Mon-Fri, noon-1am Sat)

Zortziko
GASTRONOMY €€€

9 ⊗ MAP P58, F3

Black-truffle and cod soup with squid-ink ice cream; plankton ravioli with apple-pepper gel; smoked hake cheeks with turmeric and watermelon jelly; spiced rack of lamb with anchovy sponge cake; and a chocolate sphere with almond soil and rhubarb dust are just some of the highly technical creations on this elegant Michelin-starred restaurant's no-choice tasting menus. Book well ahead. (📞944 23 97 43;

www.zortziko.es; Alameda Mazarredo 17; 7-/10-course menu €65/99; ⏱1-3.30pm & 8.30-11pm Tue-Sat)

Casa Rufo BASQUE €€

10 🍴 MAP P58, F5

Tucked in the back of a small deli and wine shop, Casa Rufo feels like a hidden dining spot – albeit one that's terrible at keeping secrets (reserve ahead). Amid shelves packed with top-quality wines, diners tuck into delectable Navarran asparagus, house-smoked duck, baked cod with tomatoes and red peppers, and chargrilled steaks. (📞944 43 21 72; www.casarufo.com; Hurtado de Amézaga 5; mains €16-20; ⏱1.30-4pm & 8.30-11pm Mon-Sat, 1.30-4pm Sun)

Nerua Guggenheim Bilbao BASQUE €€€

11 🍴 MAP P58, E1

The Museo Guggenheim Bilbao's Michelin-starred, modernist, white and ultraminimalist restaurant is under the direction of chef Josean Alija (a disciple of Ferran Adrià). Needless to say, the *nueva cocina vasca* (Basque nouvelle cuisine) is breathtaking, with multicourse extravaganzas that you'll be remembering (and perhaps paying for) long after you return home. (📞944 00 04 30; www.nerua guggenheimbilbao.com; Avenida Abandoibarra 2; 5-/9-/14-course menu €85/115/148; ⏱1-3pm Tue & Sun, 1-3pm & 8.30-10pm Wed-Sat May-Sep, 8.30-10pm Thu-Sat Oct-Apr)

El Puertito SEAFOOD €

12 🍴 MAP P58, D4

On warm summer evenings, wine-sipping crowds congregate at this small bar to enjoy an oyster or six, accompanied by a glass of crisp local white wine. Choose from a chalked-up menu of Galician, French and Portuguese oysters, served simply with a squeeze of lemon (or Tabasco sauce on request). (📞944 02 62 54; www.elpuertito.es; Calle Maestro García Rivero 9; oysters €2-4.50; ⏱10am-10pm Sun-Thu, to 11pm Fri & Sat)

Bascook BASQUE €€€

13 🍴 MAP P58, G3

Occupying a former salt warehouse, this low-lit space with exposed stone walls and elegantly set tables makes an atmospheric backdrop for high-end cooking. Chef Aitor Elizegi earns rave reviews for his modern take on Basque classics such as truffle, crab and cauliflower gratin, pork cheeks with soy-glazed sweet potato, and vegetarian options including felafel in pumpkin, broccoli and garlic broth. (📞651 931 950; www.bascook.com; Calle de Barroeta Aldamar 8; menú del día €32, tasting menús €38-62, mains €17-22; ⏱1-3.30pm Mon-Wed, 1-3.30pm & 8.30-10pm Thu-Sat; 🍴)

Yandiola BASQUE €€€

Inside Bilbao's Azkuna Zentroa (Alhóndiga) cultural centre, Yandiola (see 2 ◉ Map p58, D5) features modern

Eating & Drinking at the Basquery

Equal parts cafe, bakery, microbrewery and dining destination, the postindustrial, multiroom **Basquery** (Map p58, G4; ☑944 07 27 12; www. basquery.com; Ibañez de Bilbao 8; mains €10-15; ⏱8.30am-10pm Mon-Thu, 9am-11pm Fri & Sat, 10am-4.30pm Sun) has a stunning line-up of daily dishes, from vegan burgers to sausages with beer-and-mustard sauce, plus charcuterie and appetisers (eg sweet potato–stuffed mushrooms) that pair perfectly with the in-house IPA, golden ale and session stout. Its deli, stocking tinned fish, preserved veggies and more, is next door.

Basque and Spanish fare that is as highly touted as the strikingly redeveloped building itself. Among the many hits are fried sea nettle with chive mayonnaise, roast suckling lamb, and line-caught hake with confit egg yolk. Arrive early – or stick around afterwards – for a drink on the roof terrace. (☑944 13 36 36; www.yandiola.com; Plaza Alhóndiga 4; 3-/7-course menu €28/69, mains €19-25; ⏱1-3pm & 8.30-10.30pm)

El Huevo Frito PINTXOS €

14 ✖ MAP P58, D4

The bar at this relaxed, casual spot is laden with bright red-and-yellow Ortiz seafood tins beneath slate tiles that display its tempting array of *pintxos*. Most feature the bar's eponymous 'fried egg', such as *morcilla* (blood sausage), tempura cod with chorizo, and *jamón ibérico* (Iberian ham), each topped with a quail's egg. (☑944 41 22 49; Calle Maestro García Rivero 1; pintxos €2-4; ⏱9am-11.30pm Mon-Thu, to 12.30am Fri-Sun)

Singular PINTXOS €

15 ✖ MAP P58, F2

Amid rough-hewn stone walls, vintage iron columns, sleek industrial pipes and venting, and bare-bulbed lights, Singular lays out bite-size morsels of pure perfection on its marble-topped bar. Enjoy high-quality ingredients (grilled sardines with olive oil, sweet potato with anchovies), which you can complement with a craft brew (six on tap and another 50 by the bottle). (☑944 23 17 43; www.singularbar.com; Calle Lersundi 2; pintxos €3-4.50; ⏱9.30am-11pm Mon-Thu, to 1am Fri, 12.15pm-1am Sat)

Brass INTERNATIONAL €€

16 ✖ MAP P58, C4

This classy favourite in Bilbao's new town has a light, white, Scandinavian-style interior and a truly global palate. Its changing menu features breakfasts such as corn tortillas with avocado, banana pancakes, and chia pudding; lunch and dinner dishes including crab and coriander nachos, nasi goreng and Wagyu burger; and between-meal snacks like pistachio chocolate brownies. (www.brass27.com; Calle de Licenciado Poza 27; pintxos €2-4, mains €8-15; ⊙9am-1am Mon-Fri, 9am-2am Sat, 10am-1am Sun)

Drinking

Le Club   ROOFTOP BAR

17 🚇 MAP P58, D4

Sweeping views over Bilbao's skyline extend from this 12th-floor, glass-walled rooftop bar at the top of the Hotel Ercilla. Especially at sunset and after dark, when its decking is flooded in neon-blue light, it's a spectacular spot for a craft beer, glass of wine or dry martini, accompanied by Basque cheeses and hams, *pintxos* and

burgers. (www.hotelercilla.com; Calle de Ercilla 37-39, Hotel Ercilla; ⊙noon-midnight; 📞)

Cork   WINE BAR

18 🚇 MAP P58, C4

Taste your way around some of Spain's finest small artisan vineyards at this cosy wine bar owned and run by Jonathan García, a former Basque sommelier champion. Its blackboard chalks up 25 whites and 40 reds available by the glass. The selection of wine changes every two months but always include lightly sparkling *txakoli* and rich reds from La Rioja. (Calle de Licenciado Poza 45; ⊙11am-4pm & 7-11pm Mon-Thu, to midnight Fri & Sat)

Basque *pintxo* and beer

Gin Fizz

COCKTAIL BAR

19 MAP P58, F2

Back-lit cabinets and contemporary furnishings make this a stylish place for sipping cocktails such as its namesake, Gin Fizz (gin, sugar syrup and soda), or Pearls & Roses (jasmine and rose petal–infused gin with orange blossom water and Agua del Carmen tonic, topped with cream). Other gin infusions include green tea and liquorice,

---

Bilbao's Deusto District

Over the river from the Museo Guggenheim Bilbao, and accessible via the Pedro Arrupe footbridge, the **Universidad de Deusto** (Map p58, D1; www.deusto.es; Avenida de las Universidades 24) dominates the northern riverfront. This landmark building, initially one of Bilbao's largest, was designed by architect Francisco de Cubas in 1886 to house the Jesuit Deusto university. To the southwest of the university, Deusto is a largely residential district. But if you're in the area and fancy a bite, **Deustoarrak** (Map p58, B1; 944 75 41 54; www.deustoarrak. com; Avenida Madariaga 9; pintxos €2-3.50, mains €14-22; 9am-midnight Mon-Thu, to 2am Fri, 11am-2am Sat, to midnight Sun) is one of a number of cafes on the neighbourhood's central strip, Avenida Madariaga.

---

and dehydrated strawberries and chocolate. (www.ginfizzbilbaococktail. com; Calle Lersundi 1; 3pm-1am Wed, Thu & Sun, to 2.30am Fri & Sat)

Café Iruña

CAFE

20 MAP P58, G4

Moorish-style arches, exquisite tiling, polychrome wooden ceilings, frescoes and a marble bar are the defining characteristics of this grande dame dating from 1903. Still a wonderful place for people-watching, it works as well for afternoon coffee or an evening drink as it does for breakfast, lunch or dinner. (www.cafeirunabilbao.net; Calle de Colón de Larreátegui 13; 7.30am-1am Mon-Thu, 7.30am-1.30am Fri, 10am-2am Sat, 10am-1am Sun)

Baobab

CAFE

21 MAP P58, G4

When the rains arrive, cosy Baobab is a fine place to retreat. This riverside cafe has an excellent array of teas, infusions, beer, wine, vermouth and snacks; everything is organic and Fair Trade. Works by local artists regularly cover the walls, and there's a regular line-up of acoustic jam sessions, poetry readings and more. (www. baobabteteria.com; Calle Príncipe 1; 6-11.30pm Mon, 4-11.30pm Tue-Thu, 4pm-1am Fri, noon-1am Sat & Sun)

Residence

BAR

22 MAP P58, E2

Residence hosts acoustic jam sessions throughout the month, in-

Athletic Bilbao

Watching a football match at the **Estadio San Mamés** (Map p58, A3; www.athletic-club.eus; Calle de Licenciado Poza) is one of Bilbao's great experiences. The home side, Athletic Bilbao, is one of Spain's most successful clubs, and one of only three to have never been relegated from La Liga, along with Real Madrid and Barcelona. The club, founded in 1898 after British sailors introduced football to the city, inspires passionate local support and its traditional red and white colours are displayed in cafes and bars across town. But what sets it apart – and makes its achievements even more impressive – is its unique policy of only signing Basque players. Tickets for games are available through the team's website, directly at the stadium or, on match days, from BKK cashpoint machines.

Overlooking the river to the west of the city centre, the 2013-opened stadium has a capacity of 53,289 spectators – the largest in the Basque Country. It's within easy walking distance of the San Mamés metro station; there's a cafe and *pintxo* bar on site.

A must for all AC Bilbao fans, high-tech museum **Museo Athletic Club** (944 66 11 00; museum adult/child €10/3, incl stadium tour €14/5; 10am-8pm Tue-Sun Mar-Oct, to 7pm Tue-Sun Nov-Feb) delves into the club's legendary past, with gear and trophies dating back to 1905. Interactive touchscreens allow you to see game highlights over the last half century. For the full experience, tack on a 45-minute stadium tour (English available) that takes you to the press room, the changing rooms and out onto the pitch.

cluding Irish folk, blues and roots. Even when there's nothing on, it's a great little spot for a whisky, with more than 200 varieties to choose from, or a Manhattan cocktail and a chat with the friendly bar staff. (www.residencecafe.com; Calle Barraincua 1; 1pm-1.30am Sun-Thu, to 3am Fri & Sat)

Cotton Club CLUB
23 MAP P58, C5

A Bilbao institution since 1994, with a saxophone beer tap and bottle cap–studded walls, the Cotton Club draws a diverse crowd to its DJ-stoked nights and regular gigs – mainly jazz, blues and rock. It's a tiny place so prepare to get up close with your fellow revellers. (www. cottonclubbilbao.es; Calle de Gregorio de la Revilla 25; 8.30pm-3am Tue & Wed, to 5am Thu, to 6.30am Fri & Sat)

El Balcón de la Lola CLUB
24 MAP P58, F5

Located under the railway lines, El Balcón de la Lola doesn't get going

Bilbao's Modern Metro

Bilbao's architectural riches run deep. Walk across town and you'll come across a number of futuristic glass-and-steel constructions emerging from the ground. Nicknamed *fosteritos* after Sir Norman Foster, the British architect who designed them between 1988 and 1995, these are the entrances to the clean, cavernous stations of Bilbao's two-line metro system – a masterpiece of modern functional design.

until late. One of Bilbao's most popular mixed gay/straight clubs, this is the place to end the night if you want to keep the weekend party rolling till daybreak. It has industrial decor and packs in dance lovers – the music is mostly house. (Calle Bailén 10; ⏱11.45pm-6am Fri & Sat)

Cinnamon   CAFE

25 ⭐ MAP P58, G3

Billing itself as a 'coffee lab', Cinnamon brews organic, Basque-roasted beans in a spectrum of styles, and also serves fresh juices, smoothies, herbal and loose-leaf teas, and craft beers. Alongside its drinks list, its 'urban food' spans pastries and tortillas to salads and open-faced sandwiches. Vintage and retro furniture and fittings fill the postindustrial space. (www.facebook.com/cinnamonbilbao; Calle San Vicente 3; ⏱9.45am-4pm Mon, to 9.15pm Tue-Thu, to 11pm Fri & Sat; 📶)

Entertainment

Kafe Antzokia   LIVE MUSIC

26 ⭐ MAP P58, G3

Within a former cinema, this is the vibrant heart of contemporary Basque Bilbao, featuring international rock, blues and reggae, as well as the cream of Basque rock-pop. Weekend concerts run from 10pm to 1am, followed by DJs until 5am. During the day, it's a cafe, restaurant and cultural centre with Basque dancing classes (sign up online) all rolled into one. (📞944 24 46 25; www.kafeantzokia.eus; Calle San Vicente 2)

Teatro Campos Elíseos   THEATRE

27 ⭐ MAP P58, F5

Restored to its art-nouveau glory and modernised for contemporary productions in 2010, this show-piece was built in 1902. Today, the magnificent venue hosts plays, musicals, dance, concerts, comedy, puppet and magic shows, and occasional cinema screenings. Its multitiered main hall has a capacity of 805, while the more intimate, top-floor dome room accommodates 250 people. (📞944 43 86 10; www.teatrocampos.com; Calle de Bertendona 3)

Euskalduna Palace

LIVE MUSIC

28 ⭐ MAP P58, B2

Built on the riverside former shipyards in 1999, in a style that echoes the great shipbuilding works of the 19th century, this vast venue is home to the Bilbao Symphony Orchestra and the Basque Symphony Orchestra. With a 2164-capacity main hall and 18 smaller halls, it hosts a wide array of operas, concerts, musicals and films. (📞944 03 50 00; www.euskal duna.eus; Avenida Abandoibarra 4)

Bilborock

LIVE MUSIC

29 ⭐ MAP P58, G6

Spectacularly set in a 17th-century former church, La Merced, with soaring tiered seating and a ceiling dome, this multipurpose venue is best known for its rock, metal and pop-rock concerts. Bilborock also hosts film screenings, plays, poetry readings and creative workshops. (📞944 15 13 06; www. facebook.com/bilborockaretoa; Muelle de la Merced 1)

Back & Stage

LIVE MUSIC

30 ⭐ MAP P58, G3

This popular venue incorporates two separate spaces, Stage Live and the Back Room. Along with local and international bands, it hosts DJs and various parties; check the website to see what's on while you're here. (www.backand stage.com; Calle Uribitarte 8)

Teatro Campos Eliseos

Shopping

DendAZ

DESIGN

31 MAP P58, D5

Emerging and established Basque artists and designers showcase their works at this retail space within the Azkuna Zentroa (p60) cultural centre. Browse for contemporary clothing, including arty T-shirts, shoes and hats, as well as bags, jewellery, artworks, lamps, cabinets, ceramics and stationery. The space is regularly reconfigured to display the rotating stock, so it's worth popping in to see the latest directions in Basque design. (http://dendaz.azkunazentroa.eus; Plaza Alhóndiga 4, Azkuna Zentroa; 10am-9pm)

Chocolates de Mendaro

CHOCOLATE

32 MAP P58, D4

This old-time chocolate shop spills over with pralines, truffles and nougats in a wide variety of shapes, including anchovies and oysters. Chocolates de Mendaro also stocks its own hot chocolate mixes. It was founded in 1850 by the Saint-Gerons family, who installed a cocoa mill at their rural property, where chocolates are still made by hand today. Visits to the mill are possible by appointment. (www.chocolatesdemendaro.com; Calle de Licenciado Poza 16; 10am-2pm & 4.30-8pm Mon-Fri, 10am-2pm Sat)

Power Records

MUSIC

33 MAP P58, G4

This record shop has been a point of reference for Bilbao's vinyl lovers since the mid 1990s. Its encyclopaedic collection runs the gamut from death metal to Shirley Bassey by way of salsa, jazz, rock, pop and blues. There are LPs, posters, CDs and collectors' box sets. (www.powerrecordsbilbao.com; Calle Villarías 4; 10.30am-2pm & 4.30-8pm Mon-Sat)

Enkarterri

FOOD & DRINKS

34 MAP P58, D4

Products at this little deli are all sourced from the mountainous rural municipality of Enkarterri to Bilbao's west. Along with sourdough loaves baked daily in a wood-fired oven, it stocks cheeses, cured meats, pastries, vinegar, oils, jams, honey, wine, craft beers and chocolate. (Alameda de Urquijo 40; 10am-2.30pm & 5-8.15pm Mon-Fri, 10am-3pm Sat & Sun)

Arrese

FOOD

36 MAP P58, E4

With almost two centuries of baking experience (it opened in 1836), you'd hope the cakes at this little patisserie would taste divine, and they do – even more than expected. Treats such as *pastel vasco* (almond cream torte), *goxua* (custard-topped sponge cake) and rich chocolate truffles are among its specialities. (www.arrese.biz; Gran

Vía Lopez de Haro 24; ⏰9am-9pm Mon-Sat, 9am-3pm & 5-9pm Sun)

Persuade

FASHION & ACCESSORIES

37 🔒 MAP P58, G4

A former warehouse with timber beams, exposed brick walls and cast-iron columns makes an inspiring backdrop for browsing cutting-edge fashion by top international designers, such as Yohji Yamamoto, Daniela Gregis and Bernhard Willhelm. You'll find one-off creations, as well as vintage clothing, hats and bags. (www.persuade.es; Calle Villarías 8; ⏰11am-9pm Mon-Sat)

Market

HOMEWARES

38 🔒 MAP P58, G6

The miscellany of wares at this imaginative homewares shop includes

plant-filled terrariums, geometric ceramic pots, antique furniture, and artisan soaps and skincare products from Bilbao-based Xaboi Punpuila. (www.facebook.com/market bilbao; Calle Lamana 1; ⏰10am-1.30pm & 5-8pm Mon-Fri, 10am-2pm Sat)

Zubiarte

SHOPPING CENTRE

39 🔒 MAP P58, C2

Overlooking the river by the Deusto bridge, this impressive brick, stone and glass shopping centre was designed by US architect Robert Stern in 2004. Inside, some 50 shops include Zara, H&M and other well-known stores. Also here are a supermarket, food court and an eight-screen cinema. (www.zubiarte.com; Calle Lehendakari Leizaola 2; ⏰centre 10am-12.30am Mon-Sat, from noon Sun)

Zubiarte

FOTOKON/SHUTTERSTOCK ©

Explore
Getxo & Portugalete

It's well worth heading just outside of Bilbao to the scenic coastal enclave of Getxo, with its attractive sandy beaches, waterfront promenades and seafood eateries, plus a photogenic former fishing village. Over the Unesco-listed Puente Colgante (Vizcaya Bridge), gritty Portugalete boasts a compact medieval centre, including a striking Gothic cathedral.

The Short List

○ **Puente Colgante (p78)** Gliding across the Unesco-listed transporter bridge linking Gexto and Portugalete.

○ **Basílica de Santa María (p78)** Stepping inside Portugalete's 16th-century Gothic basilica to admire its carved altarpiece.

○ **Rialia Museo de la Industría (p78)** Delving into Portugalete's industrial past at this intriguing museum.

○ **Playa de Ereaga (p80)** Soaking up the sun on this sheltered Gexto beach.

○ **Bar Arrantzale (p83)** Sipping wine on the cobbled terrace of this bar in Puerto Viejo's atmospheric old fishing village.

Getting There & Around

Ⓜ To reach Getxo, take Metro Bilbao's Línea 1, with key stops at Areeta, Neguri and Algorta.

Ⓜ Portugalete is served by Línea 2 (Portugalete stop).

Neighbourhood Map on p76

Portugalete street and Puente Colgante (p78) AYHAN ALTUN/GETTY IMAGES ©

Walking Tour

Seaside Ramble in Getxo

An easy metro ride from Bilbao, the seaside district of Getxo offers a serene escape from the city. Clifftop views, a pretty beach and the charming, narrow lanes of an old fishing village make for an enchanting afternoon wander. There are also plenty of opportunities for snacking along the way, so come with an appetite.

Walk Facts

Start Restaurante Cubita;
Ⓜ Bidezabal

Finish San Nicolás de Bari;
Ⓜ Algorta

Length 2km; two hours

❶ Windmill

Begin your walk along this beautiful stretch of coast by admiring the windmill here, which was built to counter drought-affected watermills and was in operation from 1726 until 1787. It's now home to seafood specialist Restaurante Cubita (p82), which also has an inexpensive cafe out the front that makes an ideal spot for a coffee before setting off.

❷ Playa de Arrigunaga

Near the mouth of the Nervión estuary, the **Playa de Arrigunaga** (Algorta) is a lovely stretch of beachfront, backed by steep hillside. This is a great spot to slow down and take in the scene, with skaters zipping around on a skate park near the centre of the beach, and surfers out on the waves.

❸ Parque Usategi

High up on the cliffs above the sea, the small Parque Usategi is frequented by joggers, dog-walkers, families (there's a kids' playground) and strollers, who enjoy a quiet pocket of Getxo graced with sea breezes. It overlooks Jeffrey's Surf Spot, a favourite with local surfers thanks to waves of up to 3m (conditions permitting).

❹ Puerto Viejo

Puerto Viejo (p85) feels like a vestige of another era. Steep, narrow lanes skirt past stone cottages decorated with brightly painted shutters and balconies draped with hanging plants. Once the domain of sailors and fisherfolk, the small seaside community remains tightly knit, with children playing in the streets and old friends gathering over drinks at sundown.

❺ Txomin Taberna

Wander through the atmospheric lanes of Puerto Viejo to find neighbourhood charmer **Txomin Taberna** (Calle Ribera 43, Algorta; ⏰noon-midnight). Try a Sarracena wheat beer, made by local microbrewer Tito Blas, along with tasty *pintxos* (croquettes, anchovies, mussels in tomato salsa).

❻ Plaza de San Nicolás

Away from the seafront, the Plaza de San Nicolás is one of the prettiest squares in Getxo. It's also a completely local scene, with a handful of outdoor cafes. It's liveliest in the afternoons, when adults gather for an aperitif, while young ones chase one another about the square.

❼ San Nicolás de Bari

Built between 1854 and 1863 by Lorenzo Fancisco de Móñiz and refurbished in 1925 in neoclassical style, **San Nicolás de Bari** (Plaza de San Nicolás, Algorta; ⏰10.30am-1pm & 5.30-7.30pm Mon-Sat), on the square's northwestern side, has a stepped belfry. It's dedicated to San Nicolás de Bari, the patron saint of sailors; an exquisite model ship hangs above the altar.

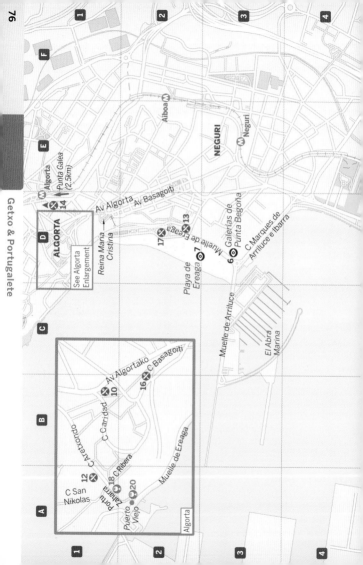

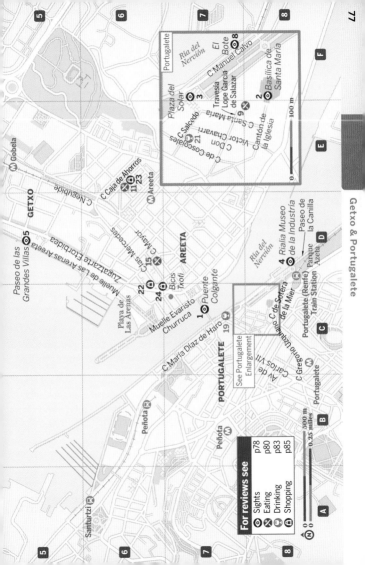

Getxo & Portugalete

For reviews see
◎ Sights	p78
✕ Eating	p80
◇ Drinking	p83
🛍 Shopping	p85

PORTUGALETE

GETXO

AREETA

See Portugalete
Enlargement

Portugalete

Ría del Nervión

Paseo de las Grandes Villas ◎5

Playa de
Las Arenas

Muelle de las Arenas Areeta

Zugatzarte Etorbidea

Puente
Colgante

Muelle Evaristo
Churruca

Bicis
Txofi

1 ◎

22 ◎   24 ◎

15 ✕

C las Mercedes

C Mayor

Caja de Ahorros
11 ◎   23 🛍
Areeta

Gobela

Neguibide

C María Díaz de Haro

Av de
Carlos VII

C Gregorio Uzquiano

Portugalete

Peñota

Peñota

Santurtzi

Portugalete (Renfe)
Train Station

C de Sotera
de la Mier

4 Rialia Museo
de la Industria

Paseo de
la Canilla

Parque
Axeta

Ría del Nervión

Portugalete

Ría del
Nervión

El
Bote 8 ◎
◎

C Manuel Calvo

Plaza del
Solar

3 ◎

Travesia
Lope García
de Salazar

C Salcedo

C Don
Victor Chavarri

C de Coscojales

21 🛍

9 ✕   C Santa María

Cantón de
la Iglesia

Basílica de
Santa María
2 ◎

19 🛍

0   100 m

0   500 m
0   0.25 miles

Sights

Puente Colgante
BRIDGE

1 ⊙ MAP P76, C7

Designed by Alberto Palacio, a disciple of Gustave Eiffel, the Unesco World Heritage–listed Puente Colgante (also known as the Vizcaya or Bizkaia Bridge) was the world's first transporter bridge, opening in 1883. The bridge, which links Getxo and Portugalete, consists of a suspended platform that sends cars and passengers gliding silently over the Ría del Nervión. You can take a lift up to the superstructure at 46m and walk across for some great, though decidedly breezy, views. (www.puente-colgante.com; per person/car one-way €0.45/1.60, walkway €8, with audio guide €10; ⊙walkway 10am-7pm Nov-Mar, to 8pm Apr-Oct)

Basílica de Santa María
BASILICA

2 ⊙ MAP P76, F8

Portugalete's impressive basilica (1580) stands atop an earlier 14th-century church that originally marked the town's highest point. A striking structure, it's largely Gothic with flying buttresses, gargoyles and austere sandstone walls; the bell tower was a later 18th-century addition. Inside, the carved wood Renaissance-era altarpiece is a highlight. (Cantón de la Iglesia, Portugalete; ⊙10.30am-1.15pm & 4.30-8pm Mon-Sat, 10.30am-1.15pm Sun mid-Jun–mid-Sep, services only rest of year)

Plaza del Solar
SQUARE

3 ⊙ MAP P76, F7

At the foot of Portugalete's medieval centre, this cobbled square makes for a fine photo with its handsome 19th-century buildings and august monument to Víctor Chávarri (1854–1900), a local industrialist, business person and politician. At the plaza's heart, an ornate bandstand provides the outdoor stage for regular Sunday performances by the local brass band. (Portugalete)

Rialia Museo de la Industría
MUSEUM

4 ⊙ MAP P76, D8

Learn about Portugalete's industrial history at this small waterfront museum. Displays, which include paintings, models and machinery parts, chart the town's development and the effect early industrialisation had on the area's landscape and social make-up. Best of all are the short films showing fiery industrial action – smelting, welding, molten flows – backed by dramatic musical arrangements. (📞944 72 43 84; www.rialia.net; Paseo de la Canilla, Portugalete; adult/child €2/free; ⊙10am-2.30pm Tue-Thu, 10am-2pm & 5-7pm Fri & Sat, 10.30am-3pm Sun Apr-Sep, 9.30am-1.30pm Tue & Wed, 9.30am-1.30pm & 3-5pm Thu & Fri, 10am-3pm Sat & Sun Oct-Mar)

Paseo de las Grandes Villas

AREA

5 ◉ MAP P76, D5

The Paseo is the unofficial name given to Getxo's seafront – made up of Muelle de Las Arenas Areeta and Calle Marques de Arriluce e Ibarra. The 'Villas' part of the name is a reference to the extravagant mansions that pepper the route, many of which date to the town's heyday in the early 20th century. Two to look out for are the 1911-built **Casa Cisco** (Zugatzarte Etorbidea 61) and turreted, early 20th-century **Lezama-Legizamón** (Calle Marques de Arriluce e Ibarra). (Getxo)

Galerías de Punta Begoña

LANDMARK

6 ◉ MAP P76, D3

This massive stone structure was built in 1919 as a continuation of Getxo's defensive wall. It's an impressive sight, complete with columns and a balustraded terrace, though it's in a bad state of decay. Long-term restoration, however, is underway. And while it's not open to the public, free one-hour guided visits in Basque and Spanish are offered throughout the year, with some English-language tours in August. (☏ 635 717 333; www.punta begonagetxo.eus; Muelle de Ereaga, Getxo; ⏱ guided tours by reservation)

View of Portugalete from Puente Colgante

Playa de Ereaga

BEACH

7 ⊙ MAP P76, D2

Ideal for families, this long, sheltered sandy beach runs between the Galerías de Punta Begoña and Puerto Viejo. You can hire sunbeds and parasols (per day €3.50). Beach football tournaments take place here in summer. (Getxo)

El Bote

CRUISE

8 ⊙ MAP P76, F7

El Bote runs a circular hop-on, hop-off route from Portugalete, passing under the Puente Colgante (p78), up to Santurtzi (on the Nervión's west bank), across to Getxo's El Abra Marina and back. Multilingual audio guides are included. It sails four times per day, with the first departure at 11am. There are also *pintxo* cruises and longer cruises to Bilbao. (📞605 014 365; www.elbotebilbao.com; Calle Manuel Calvo, Portugalete; 24hr ticket €8; ⏱Mon-Fri Apr-Sep, Sat & Sun year-round)

Eating

Restaurante Torre de Salazar

BASQUE €€

9 ✕ MAP P76, E7

In a 15th-century tower that was rebuilt in the mid-20th century, market-fresh seafood is accompanied by picturesque views over the Puente Colgante from its glass-walled dining room. As well as grilled John Dory or sardines, and octopus with sweet red pepper pu-

rée, it serves meat dishes such as Iberian pork cheeks stewed in La Rioja red wine sauce. (📞944 07 70 94; www.torredesalazar.com; Travesía Lope Garcia de Salazar, Portugalete; mains €17-21.50; ⏱1.30-4.30pm Tue & Wed, 1.30-4.30pm & 8.30-11pm Thu-Sat, 1-6pm Sun)

Tellagorri

PINTXOS €€

10 ✕ MAP P76, B1

An 1863-built farmhouse with stone walls and timber beams now houses this all-purpose venue. Opening to a charming umbrella-shaded terrace, the ground-floor bar serves stunning *pintxos* (mini cod tacos, pork belly with green peppers...) and larger dishes (octopus burgers and chargrilled steaks are highlights). Upstairs, the formal dining room has refined Basque cuisine at lunch and dinner (three-course menus €35). (Avenida Basgoiti Hiribidea 62, Algorta; pintxos €2-3.50, mains €9-18; ⏱10am-11.30pm Tue-Sun; 📶)

Tudelilla

BASQUE €€

11 ✕ MAP P76, E6

Hidden away on a backstreet, this traditional restaurant is a local favourite. And with its outdoor tables, inviting wood-beamed interior and choice of locally caught fish and *solomillo* (sirloin) steaks, it hits the mark perfectly. A bargain €11 daily *menú* is served at lunchtime from Monday to Friday. (📞944 64 08 82; Calle Caja de Ahorros 12, Areeta; mains €14-22; ⏱1-4pm Mon, 1-4pm & 9-11pm Tue-Sat)

A Basque History Lesson

No one quite knows where the Basque people came from (they have no migration myth in their oral history), but their presence here is believed to predate even the earliest known migrations. The Romans left the hilly Basque Country more or less to itself, but the expansionist Castilian crown gained sovereignty over Basque territories during the Middle Ages (1000–1450), although with considerable difficulty; Navarra constituted a separate kingdom until 1512. Even when they came within the Castilian orbit, Navarra and the three other Basque provinces (Guipúzcoa, Vizcaya and Álava) extracted broad autonomy arrangements, known as the *fueros* (the ancient laws of the Basques).

After the Second Carlist War in 1876, all provinces except Navarra were stripped of their coveted *fueros,* thereby fuelling nascent Basque nationalism. Yet, although the Partido Nacionalista Vasco (PNV; Basque Nationalist Party) was established in 1894, support was never uniform as all Basque provinces included a considerable Castilian contingent.

When the Republican government in Madrid proposed the possibility of home rule (self-government) to the Basques in 1936, both Guipúzcoa and Vizcaya took up the offer. When the Spanish Civil War erupted, conservative rural Navarra and Álava supported Franco, while Vizcaya and Guipúzcoa sided with the Republicans, a decision they paid a high price for in the four decades that followed.

It was during the Franco days that Euskadi Ta Askatasuna (ETA; Basque Homeland and Freedom) was first born. It was originally set up to fight against the Franco regime, which suppressed the Basques through banning the language and almost all forms of Basque culture. After Franco's death, ETA called for nothing less than total independence and continued its bloody fight against the Spanish government until, in October 2011, the group announced a 'definitive cessation of its armed activity'.

Today, while ETA is no longer active, there is still a peaceful but strong sense of nationalism, and you'll often see banners, posters and signs emblazoned with the words *Euskal Herriak Independentzia* (Basque Country Independence) throughout the region.

Karola Etxea

SEAFOOD €€€

12 🍴 MAP P76, A1

The blue-trimmed, wood-beamed dining room of this Puerto Viejo restaurant, atmospherically housed in a picture-perfect white fisher's cottage, sets the stage for delicacies such as fresh prawns, chargrilled octopus, hake and clams in green sauce, and steamed *percebe* (goose barnacles). While seafood is the speciality, there are also a couple of daily meat dishes. (📞 944 60 08 68; www.karolaetxea. net; Calle Aretxondo 22, Algorta; mains €20-27; ⏰ 1-4pm & 9-11pm)

Tamarises Izarra

BASQUE €€€

13 🍴 MAP P76, D2

Basque chef Javier Izarra's creative contemporary cuisine earns him rave reviews. At his smart beachside premises' formal upstairs restaurant and sunny sea-facing terrace, you can dine on innovative creations such as foie gras tacos or roast scallops with mushroom custard, followed by cod with black-garlic *pil-pil* sauce, finishing off with nougat soufflé with bee-pollen ice cream. (📞 944 91 00 05; www. tamarisesizarra.com; Muelle de Ereaga 4, Getxo; mains €16-26; ⏰ 1-4pm & 8pm-midnight Mon-Sat, 1-4pm Sun)

Restaurante Cubita

SEAFOOD €€€

14 🍴 MAP P76, D1

Built into Getxo's only windmill, dating from 1726 and overlook-ing the Playa de Arrigunaga, this much-lauded restaurant specialises in top-of-the-line seafood: tempura squid with squid-ink aioli, roast grouper with crab and prawn bisque, or clams steamed in *txakoli* (white wine). Wine buffs will also enjoy the formidable list of largely Spanish and French labels. (📞 944 91 17 00; www.restaurantecubita.com; Carretera de Galea 30, Algorta; mains €17-35; ⏰ 1-4pm & 8.30-11.30pm Mon, Tue & Thu-Sat, 1-4pm Wed & Sun)

La Kazuela

BASQUE €€

15 🍴 MAP P76, D6

Near the historic Puente Colgante transporter bridge, this lively bar-restaurant is popular for *pintxos* – the salmon and Cantabrian anchovy creations are excellent – and more substantial mains, such as chargrilled sea bream or veal steaks. (📞 946 08 06 02; www.lakazuela.com; Calle Mayor 17, Areeta; pintxos €2-4, mains €10.50-17; ⏰ 7am-midnight Mon-Fri, 8am-1am Sat, to midnight Sun)

Satistegi

SEAFOOD €€

16 🍴 MAP P76, B2

Revel in sweeping sea views and excellent seafood at this contemporary bar-restaurant in Algorta. The blond-wood interior, with herringbone floors, high tables and black-and-white photos of Getxo, is a relaxed spot to linger over *pintxos* from the marble bar or larger dishes, such as a platter of grilled prawns or fried calamari, and a bottle of wine. (📞 944 36 28

58; www.facebook.com/satistegi; Calle Basagoiti 51, Algorta; pintxos €2-4.50, mains €14-26.50; ⏰9am-11pm)

Brasserie Igeretxe

BASQUE €€€

17 ✗ MAP P76, D2

Views of the beach, bay and hills beyond extend from the dining room and terrace of this fine-dining restaurant inside the landmark Hotel Igeretxe. *Marmitako* (Basque fish stew with tuna, clams and red peppers), pig's trotters from Deba on the Central Basque Coast sautéed in local cider, and raspberry sponge with apple and *txakoli* sorbet are among its menu highlights. (📞944 91 00 09; www.brasserie-igeretxe.com; Muelle de

Ereaga 3, Getxo; mains €18-24; ⏰1.30-4pm & 8.30-11pm Mon-Sat, 1.30-4pm Sun; 📶)

Drinking

Bar Arrantzale

BAR

18 🍺 MAP P76, A1

With its delightful plane tree–shaded cobbled terrace cooled by the afternoon sea breeze and its charming setting in Getxo's whitewashed Puerto Viejo, this laid-back bar is a top spot to slow down over a glass of wine or beer. Nibble on *pintxos* – the *morcillas* (blood sausages) and cod-stuffed peppers are excellent – or a plate of the house speciality, calamari. (www.arrantzale.com; Portu Zaharra 3, Algorta; ⏰noon-11pm)

Traditional Basque *pintxos*

Exploring Punta Galea

Walking path **Paseo de Punta Galea** runs for 6km around the Punta Galea, the cliff-bound promontory that juts into the sea north of Getxo, characterised by its exposed rock strata and white cliffs similar to those of Normandy, France, and Dover, England.

At the path's southern end is the 18th-century windmill now housing Restaurante Cubita (p82); 1km north are the remains of Fuerte de La Galea, a defensive fort dating from 1742.

The path's northernmost point is Playa Salvaje, where you'll often see airborne paragliders. If you're keen to take to the skies yourself, book a tandem paragliding flight with **Parapente** (☏607 213 431; www.parapentesopelana.com; Avenida Arrietara 85, Sopelana; 20min paraglide adult/child €55/45; ☉by appointment) for spectacular aerial views of the coast's geological formations and beaches.

For a quick return to Getxo (and Bilbao), hop on Metro Bilbao's Línea 1 at Larrabasterra, 1.2km southeast of Playa Salvaje.

Gran Hotel Puente Colgante

BAR

 19 MAP P76, C7

Grab a drink and take a seat on the terrace of the Gran Hotel Puente Colgante. You'll be perfectly positioned to admire views of the famous bridge and watch the world stroll past on the waterfront promenade, while enjoying an Amer Picon Basque cocktail (bittersweet orange liqueur, grenadine, brandy and soda water). (www.puente colganteboutiquehotel.com; Calle María Díaz de Haro 2, Portugalete; ☉8am-11pm Mon-Thu & Sun, 9am-midnight Fri & Sat)

Portu Zaharra Bar

PUB

20 MAP P76, A2

Park yourself on the steps at Getxo's Puerto Viejo alongside this traditional white-and-green cottage and take in the sea views, while sampling the local tipple of choice, txakoli, a glass of sagardoa (cider) or an ice-cold Basque craft beer. (www.portuzaharra.com; Portu Zaharra 35, Algorta; ☉10am-11pm Sun-Thu, to midnight Fri & Sat)

Casa Vicente

BAR

21 MAP P76, E7

Portugalete's unrivalled nightlife spot, Casa Vicente packs in the garrulous beer- and cocktail-loving crowds on weekends. It's hidden in the old lanes just up from the seafront, and is well worth seeking out any time for its quality pintxos, fine drink selections (try a vermouth) and ambient tunes. (Calle Salcedo 3, Portugalete; ☉10am-3.30pm & 6pm-midnight Mon-Fri, noon-4pm & 6pm-2am Sat & Sun)

Shopping

Ana Valladares
FASHION & ACCESSORIES

22 🅿 MAP P76, C6

Renowned local fashion designer Ana Valladares creates highly distinctive, ultra-stylish women's fashion incorporating straight lines and unusual prints, as well as bags, scarves and hats, here in Getxo. Garments can be altered in-house. (www.facebook.com/anavalladaresque moda; Calle las Mercedes 9, Areeta; ⏱10.30am-2pm & 5-8pm Mon-Sat)

Aingara
GIFTS & SOUVENIRS

23 🅿 MAP P76, E6

Shelves at this sweet neighbourhood shop brim with great gift ideas: jewellery with ancient Basque symbols; baseball hats and berets with those iconic red-and-green flags; 'Euskal Herria' (Basque Country) tea towels; and clothing (for men, women and children) that would make you feel right at home in a Basque culture fest. (www.bordadosaingara.com/es/bordados-aingara; Calle Caja de Ahorros 18, Areeta; ⏱10am-2pm & 4.30-8.30pm Mon-Fri, 10am-2pm Sat)

La Granja
FOOD & DRINKS

24 🅿 MAP P76, C6

Founded in 1965, this much-loved deli has all the essentials for assembling a first-rate picnic: wines,

Cycling in Getxo

Getxo's waterfront path is great for a spin, stretching 4km from just south of the Puente Colgante (p78) transporter bridge to Algorta's old port area, **Puerto Viejo** (Map p76, A2; Algorta).

Hire wheels from **Bicis Txofi** (Map p76, C7; 📞944 64 83 81; Calle Paulino Mendivil 5, Areeta; bike hire for hour/day €7/30; ⏱10am-1.30pm & 4.30-8pm Mon-Fri, 10am-1.30pm Sat), which can get you outfitted with a decent hybrid bike. Alternatively, take advantage of Getxo's inexpensive bike-sharing network, **GetxoBizi** (www.getxobizi.com; per day €2; ⏱7am-10pm). This has 13 stations scattered around the area, including one half a block north of the Puente Colgante. A day pass allows unlimited rentals in increments of one hour; you'll have to register online (it's easy), and you'll need a mobile phone with you in order to check out a bike.

cheeses, hams, olive oils, fresh breads, antipasti, chocolates, tins of smoked fish and more. (www.lagranjaseleccion.es; Calle Amistad 15, Areeta; ⏱9am-2pm & 5-8pm Mon-Fri, 9.15am-2.30pm Sat & Sun)

Worth a Trip 🔭
Understand the Past at Gernika

A name synonymous with the brutality of the Spanish Civil War, Gernika (Spanish: Guernica) suffered a devastating bombing raid that levelled the city in 1937. That harrowing April day left a deep mark on the city's identity. Following the war, Gernika was quickly reconstructed, and today excellent museums deal with the bombing and indestructibility of Basque culture through the ages.

Gernika is an easy day trip from Bilbao by Euskotren train from Atxuri train station (€3.40, one hour). Trains run every half-hour; buses also make the journey.

Museo de la Paz de Gernika

Gernika's seminal experience is a visit to the **Gernika Peace Museum** (☎946 27 02 13; www.museodelapaz.org; Plaza Foru 1; adult/child €5/free, Sun free; ☯10am-7pm Tue-Sat, 10am-2pm Sun Mar-Oct, 10am-2pm & 4-6pm Tue-Sat, 10am-2pm Sun Nov, Dec & Feb), where audiovisual displays reveal the horror of war in the Basque Country and worldwide. On nearby Calle Allende Salazar is a ceramic-tile version of Picasso's *Guernica*.

Museo de Euskal Herría

Housed in the beautiful 18th-century Palacio de Montefuerte, the **Museum of the Basque Country** (☎946 25 54 51; www.bizkaikoa.bizkaia.eus; Calle Allende Salazar 5; adult/child €3.50/2; ☯10am-2pm & 4-7pm Tue-Sat, 10.30am-2.30pm Sun) illustrates Basque history through old maps, engravings and other documents and portraits.

Parque de los Pueblos de Europa

The city's most elegant **park** (Calle Allende Salazar) contains a monumental work by renowned Basque sculptor Eduardo Chillida. Adjacent is the Tree of Gernika, under which the Basque parliament met from medieval times to 1876.

Nearby: Cuevas de Santimamiñe

Located 6.5km northeast of Gernika, the walls of this **cave system** (☎944 65 16 57; www.santimamiñe.com; Basondo; adult/child €5/free; ☯10am-5.30pm mid-Apr–mid-Oct, to 1pm Tue-Sun mid-Oct–mid-Apr) are decorated with around 50 different Neolithic paintings depicting bison, horses, rhinos and the like. To protect these delicate artworks, only reproductions are on display. Tours lasting 90 minutes take place on the hour. Call ahead to reserve an English-speaking guide.

★ Top Tips

Within the 220-sq-km bird-filled Urdaibai Biosphere Reserve, the **Urdaibai Bird Center** (☎946 25 11 57; www.birdcenter.org; Orueta Auzoa 7, Gautegiz-Arteaga; adult/child €5/2; ☯11am-7pm Jul & Aug, to 4pm Tue-Fri, to 7pm Sat & Sun Mar-Jun, Sep & Oct, to 5pm Fri-Sun Nov-Feb) is 5.5km northeast of Gernika. Your own wheels are the easiest way to reach this sight.

✗ Take a Break

Top-notch *pintxo* bars concentrate on and around Calle Pablo Picasso; **Auzokoa** (www.facebook.com/AuzokoaTaberna; Calle Pablo Picasso 9; pintxos €2-3; ☯8am-4pm & 7-11pm) is a standout.

Central Basque Coast

The coastline between Bilbao and San Sebastián has spectacular seascapes, with cove after cove of sun-dappled waves and verdant fields suddenly ending where cliffs plunge into the sea, along with pretty beaches, scenic coastal walks and fabulous seafood.

The Short List

○ **Getaria (p90)** *Exploring this enchanting medieval fishing village's historic streets, fashion museum and superb seafood restaurants.*

○ **San Juan de Gaztelugatxe (p93)** *Making a pilgrimage to this rocky isle topped by a hermitage – one of the most photogenic sights in the Basque Country.*

○ **Basque Coast Geopark (p98)** *Discovering the coastline's dramatic cliffs and astonishing rock formations on foot or by boat.*

○ **Crusoe Treasure (p94)** *Tasting vintages from the world's first underwater winery on land or out at sea.*

○ **Mundaka (p94)** *Riding the legendary waves at Mundaka.*

Getting There & Around

🚗 Most travellers explore by car; hire companies are located in San Sebastián and Bilbao.

🚌 Regular services run from San Sebastián via the coast to Lekeitio (€7.25, 1½ hours). Bilbao has services via Bermeo (€2.55, 50 minutes) to Mundaka (€2.55, one hour). Travelling between Lekeitio and Mundaka (€2.85, one hour) requires a change inland in Gernika.

Neighbourhood Map on p92

Coastal path on San de Juan Gaztelugatxe (p93)

Top Experience 📷
Discover Coastal Basque Lifestyle in Getaria

The medieval fishing settlement of Getaria is a world away from nearby cosmopolitan San Sebastián and is a wonderful place to get a feel for coastal Basque culture. The old village tilts gently downhill to a tiny harbour and a short but very pleasant beach, almost totally sheltered from all but the heaviest Atlantic swells.

◎ MAP P92, D3

Buses run regularly from San Sebastián to Getaria (€2.65, one hour). From Bilbao, you'll need to change in Zarautz to reach Getaria (€9.40, 1¼ hours).

Cristóbal Balenciaga Museoa

Although Getaria is mainly about sun, sand and seafood, don't miss a visit to the **Cristóbal Balenciaga Museoa** (📞 943 00 88 40; www. cristobalbalenciagamuseoa.com; Aldamar Parkea 6; adult/child €10/7; ⏱10am-8pm Jul & Aug, to 7pm Tue-Sun Mar-Jun, Sep & Oct, to 3pm Tue-Sun Nov-Feb). Local son Cristóbal became a giant in the fashion world in the 1950s and '60s, and this impressive museum showcases some of his best works. Start with a 23-minute video (English version available) that gives an overview of the fashion innovator once viewed as the king of couture. Afterwards, wander through the futuristic galleries, where artfully lit displays showcase pieces from his wide-ranging collection, including his Infanta gown, inspired by costumes worn by Spanish princesses as painted by Diego Velázquez.

Iglesia de San Salvador

With its unusual shape, sloping wooden floors, and nautical atmosphere, Getaria's striking 1397-built Gothic **church** (Calle Nagusia 39; ⏱9.30am-7pm) is well worth a stop. Features worth noting include the gravestone of the great navigator Juan Sebastián Elcano, who was baptised here, and an underground passage (Katrapona, not open to the public) that leads to Getaria's harbour.

El Ratón

At the end of the harbour is a forested former island known as El Ratón (the Mouse), which was attached via a breakwater in the 15th century. Perhaps it was this giant mouse that first encouraged the town's most famous son, the sailor Juan Sebastián Elcano, to take to the ocean. In the early 16th century, he became the first person to complete a circumnavigation of the globe, after Magellan, the captain of his ship, died halfway through the endeavour.

★ Top Tips

○ Dining is a big part of the Getaria experience. Be sure to reserve ahead, even at lunchtime.

○ Produced by vineyards on the surrounding hillsides, *txakoli* pairs perfectly with seafood.

○ Bring your walking shoes. There are some lovely strolls in the area, including the path up El Ratón.

✕ Take a Break

With a 'fin-to-tail' ethos, seafood specialist **Elkano** (📞 943 14 00 24; www. restauranteelkano. com; Calle Herrerieta 2; mains €26-39; ⏱1-3.45pm & 8-11pm Wed-Sat, 1-3.45pm Sun & Mon) is famed for its grilled whole turbot.

Dine on catches landed at the harbour in front of **Txoko Getaria** (📞 943 14 05 39; www. txokogetaria.com; Calle Katrapona 5; mains €19-27; ⏱12.30-4pm & 7.30-11.30pm).

Central Basque Coast

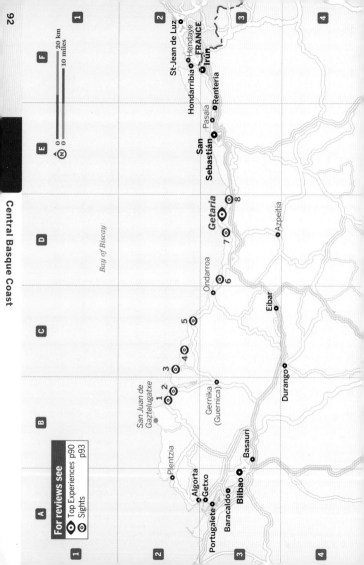

For reviews see
◉ Top Experiences p90
◎ Sights   p93

20 km
10 miles

Ⓔ
Ⓝ

Bay of Biscay

FRANCE
St-Jean de Luz
Hendaye
Hondarribia
Irún
Pasaia
Renteria
San
Sebastián
Getaria
◉ 8
◉ 7
◉ 6
Ondarroa
Azpeitia
Eibar
◉ 5
◉ 4
◉ 3
◉ 2
◉ 1
San Juan de
Gaztelugatxe
Plentzia
Gernika
(Guernica)
Durango
Basauri
Algorta
Getxo
Bilbao
Baracaldo
Portugalete

Bermeo

1 ◉ MAP P92, B2

This fishing port 35km northeast of Bilbao is refreshingly down to earth and hasn't lost its soul to tourism. There's much history hidden in its laneways, as some centuries ago Bermeo was a centre of the whaling industry. Scenic outlooks offer memorable views over the rugged seashore, although the only beaches in the area are rocky and wave-battered.

One of the most photographed features of the Basque coast, 10km to Bermeo's northwest, is the small, rocky isle of **San Juan de Gaztelugatxe** (Map p92, B2; www.tiketa.eus/gaztelugatxe; island free, hermitage €1; ◷ island year-round, hermitage 11am-6pm Tue-Sat, to 3pm Sun Jul & Aug). Accessed from the mainland by climbing 241 steps via a stone footbridge, it's topped by a hermitage, Ermita de San Juan de Gaztelugatxe, which was built by the Knights Templar in the 10th century. Between Easter and September, island entry is only guaranteed by reserving an allocated time slot ahead of time online. Local tradition holds that it was named after St John the Baptist, who allegedly visited the island.

Small but absorbing, Bermeo's **Arrantzaleen Museoa** (Museo de Pescadores; ☎ 946 88 11 71; www.face book.com/arrantzaleenmuseoa; Torre de Ercilla; adult/child €3/free; ◷ 10am-2pm & 4-7pm Tue-Sat, to 2pm Sun) has model ships, shipbuilding tools

Ermita de San Juan de Gaztelugatxe

and implements such as harpoons that provide an overview of the history of Basque fishing. It spans the lives, work and customs of fishers, and boats and techniques throughout the centuries, as well as a small section covering the Basque naval forces. It's located in the 15th-century Torre de Ercilla; displays also cover the history of the tower itself. Signage is in Basque and Spanish; an English-language leaflet is available.

Everyone's favourite restaurant in Bermeo is humble-looking, family-run **Artza** (946 02 93 71; Askatasun Bidea 1; 3-course menu weekday/weekend €12/20; 1-4pm & 7-10.30pm), just across from the port, which churns out mouth-watering plates of grilled

octopus, tuna and skate, and an outstanding *marmitaco* (hearty fish soup). On busy summer days and on weekends reservations are essential.

Mundaka

2 MAP P92, B2

Home to one of the best left-hand waves in Europe, with 200m-plus rides and deep barrels, Mundaka is a legendary name for surfers across the world. Mundaka is also a resolutely Basque port with a pretty main square and harbour area.

From March to October, **Mundaka Surf Shop** (946 17 72 29; www.mundakasurfshop.com; Paseo Txorrokopunta 10; 2-hour surf lesson €30, surfboard per 2 hours/half day €15/25, SUP or kayak per 2 hours/half day €18/40; 10am-9pm Jul & Aug, 10.30am-1.30pm & 5-8pm Mon-Fri, 10.30am-2pm & 5-8pm Sat, 11am-2pm Sun Sep-Jun) runs a reputable surf school, and leads guided one-hour SUP board tours along the river (€50). You can hire gear year-round, including surf and SUP boards, kayaks, bodyboards and wetsuits. Lessons take place on scenic beach **Playa de Laida** on the eastern side of the estuary (a 23km drive or a mere 200m-or-so paddle from Mundaka).

Elantxobe

3 MAP P92, C2

Located 14km west of Lekeitio, the tiny hamlet of Elantxobe, with its colourful houses clasping like

Underwater Winery

The world's first underwater winery, **Crusoe Treasure** (944 01 50 40; www.underwaterwine.com; Areatza Hiribidea, Plentzia; on-land tastings from €40, 3hr boat trip €262; by appointment), ages its vintages 20m below the surface on an artificial reef. Tastings of its whites and reds are available on land at its tasting room. For a truly immersive experience, take a scenic boat ride out to the reef, where barnacle-encrusted bottles are hauled up for you to taste. Swimming off the boat is possible; prices also include *pintxos*.

geckos to an almost sheer cliff face, is undeniably one of the most picturesque spots along the entire coast. There's no beach here, but it's a pretty place to explore, and on hot days you can join the local children jumping into the sea from the harbour walls. Take care on the walk, as it's a very steep descent from the main road to the waterfront.

Ea

4 ◉ MAP P92, C2

Water surrounds the photogenic little village of Ea, 10km west of Lekeitio. Sitting at the head of a narrow estuary, the colourful lanes of the 16th-century village are linked by humpbacked medieval bridges. At the seaward end of the village is a sandy patch of beach.

Near the river mouth, **Sokaire** (☏ 688 604 690; www.facebook.com/sokaire.Ea; Calle Kaibidea 4; 2hr kayak/SUP board hire €16/17, excursions from €20; ☉ 10am-8pm Jul-Sep) hires out kayaks and SUP boards, and leads excursions. You can go snorkelling, head out on a two-hour kayaking trip to nearby caves, or take part in 'coasteering', which entails a bit of trekking, climbing, jumping from cliffs and swimming. Outside of the summer season, contact the company in advance for rentals.

Ea is the starting point for several scenic walks in the area, ranging from 5km to 7km. Among the most scenic is the 5km Sendero de las Letanías. This well-marked path begins near the church and heads up to Bedarona for marvellous views, before descending towards the rugged coastline and looping back to Ea. Stop by the seasonal **tourist office** (☏ 688 864 654; www.eaturismo.com; Donibane Enparantza 2; ☉ 10am-7pm Jul & Aug, to 2pm & 4-7pm Mon-Sat, to 2pm Sun Easter holidays) for a map and trail info. When it's closed, pick up maps at tourist offices in Bilbao, Getaria or San Sebastián.

On Ea's main square, lively **Eskoikiz Jatetxea** (☏ 946 27 59 73; Plaza Donibane; pintxos €1.50-3, 3-course menu weekday/weekend €12/15; ☉ 1-3.30pm & 8-11pm Tue-Sun) serves delicious *pintxos* (its anchovy tortillas and crab-stuffed Gernika green peppers are highlights) and traditional Basque dishes, such as *alubias* (blood sausage and black-bean stew), *txipirones* (baby squid cooked in its own ink) and *txuleta* (char-grilled steak served super-rare). Cash only.

Lekeitio

5 ◉ MAP P92, C2

Bustling Lekeitio is gorgeous. The attractive old core is centred on the **Basílica de la Asunción de Santa María** (www.basilicadelekeitio.com; Calle Abaroa; ☉ 8am-noon & 5-7.30pm Mon-Fri). This grand late-Gothic church, complete with flying buttresses topped with pinnacles, offers a vision of grandeur surprising for such a small town. In fact, Lekeitio's prolific whaling industry helped fund such

Basque Sports

The national sport of the Basque country is *pelota basque* (aka *jai alai*), and every village in the region has its own *fronton* (court) – often backing up against the village church. Pelota can be played in several different ways: bare-handed, with small wooden rackets, or with a long hand-basket called a *chistera*, with which the player can throw the ball at speeds of up to 300km/h. It's possible to see pelota matches throughout the region during summer. One place where you can get a primer is **Miruaitz Taberna** (☏634 426 588; www.facebook.com/miruaitztabernamutriku; Calle Sabanika; ⏰9am-11pm), next to the village *fronton* in Mutriku. Juanjo, a player in the former US pro teams, now coaches the next generation, while his wife Caterina runs the cafe. Games take place on Fridays from around 7pm, except during August.

Basque sports aren't just limited to pelota: there's also log cutting, stone lifting, bale tossing and tug of war. Most stemmed from the day-to-day activities of the region's farmers and fisherfolk, and are kept alive at numerous fiestas.

extravagance. Highlights include the frieze-covered west facade, and a Gothic-Flemish altarpiece that's the third-largest in Spain after Seville and Toledo.

Lekeitio's busy harbour is lined by multicoloured, half-timbered old buildings – some of which house fine seafood restaurants and *pintxo* bars. On a clifftop 1.8km north of the centre, the scenic **Santa Catalina** (☏946 84 40 17; www.faro-lekeitio.com; Santa Katalina Ibilbidea; adult/child €6/4.50; ⏰visits 11.30am, 1pm, 4.30pm & 6pm Wed-Sat, 11.30am & 1pm Sun Jul & Aug, weekends only Sep-Jun) lighthouse contains an interpretation centre that gives a lively overview of coastal navigation and challenges for Basque fishermen. But for most visitors, it's the beaches that are the main draw.

One of the great attractions of Lekeitio is the rocky island of **Isla de San Nicolás**, known in Basque as Garraitz, sitting just offshore of the main beach (Playa Isuntza). When the tides are low a paved path appears, allowing visitors to stroll straight out to the island, and take a 200m trail to the top for a fine view over the seaside. Be mindful of the tides, so you don't have to swim back! The **tourist office** (☏946 84 40 17; www.lekeitio. org; Plaza Independencia; ⏰10am-2pm & 4-8pm Jul & Aug, to 2pm Tue-Sun Sep-Jun) posts tidal charts.

Situated 800m south of the centre, **Mesón Arropain** (☏946 24 31 83; Iñigo Arrieta Etorbidea 5;

mains €23-28; ⏱1-3.30pm & 8-11pm Jun-Aug, 1-3.30pm & 8-10.30pm Fri & Sat, 1-3.30pm Sun Sep-May) serves some of the best seafood for miles around. The chef lets the high-quality ingredients speak for themselves in simple but beautifully prepared dishes. Start off with its famous *arrain zopa* (fish soup) and move on to *zapo beltza* (deep-sea anglerfish with fried Gernika peppers) or *legatzen kokotxak* (hake with prawns and clams). There's an excellent wine selection.

Mutriku

6 ⊚ MAP P92, D3

A fishing town through and through, Mutriku, which dates from the early 13th century, is tightly wedged between slices of steep hills. It's an attractive village of tall houses painted in blues and greens and steps that tumble steeply downwards to the port. There's a small beach on the outskirts with two natural sea pools, a major draw on hot sunny days. Scenic trails go 4.5km west to Saturraran and 15km east through the Basque Coast Geopark (p98) via the beachside village of Deba all the way to Zumaia.

Zumaia

7 ⊚ MAP P92, D3

Where the Urola and Narrondo rivers converge, the industrial port town of Zumaia has a charming centre and two popular beaches located along the world's longest stretch of flysch sedimentary rock

Playa de Itzurun (p98), Zumaia

strata. On the town's western side, **Playa de Itzurun** is wedged in among cliffs where fossils in the rock include ammonites. On the eastern side of the estuary, 2.5km east of Playa de Itzurun, is a more traditional stretch of sand, **Playa de Santiago**. The village is also a gateway to the wondrous cliffs of the **Basque Coast Geopark** (www. geoparkea.com), a geological wonder spanning 60 million years.

Zarautz

8 ⊙ MAP P92, D3

Zarautz consists of a 2.5km-long soft sand beach (the Basque Country's longest) backed by a largely modern strip of tower blocks. The beach has some of the best surfing in the area and there are a number of surf schools, including **Moor Surf Eskola** (☎943 02 08 94; www.moorsurfeskola. com; Calle Nafarroa 11; 90min lesson €32, surfboard hire per 1/2/4 hours €10/15/20; ⊙9am-9pm Jul & Aug, to 7pm Apr-Jun, Sep & Oct, to 5pm Nov-Mar). On the promenade overlooking the beach, it runs a variety of lessons for all levels of ability overseen by professional instructors, and hires out boards and wetsuits.

It's well worth detouring from the sands to explore the tangle of medieval streets. On one of its liveliest little lanes, Zarautz's 1903-opened **market** (Calle Nagusia 27; ⊙8.15am-1.15pm & 5-8.15pm Mon-Fri, 8am-1.30pm Sat) is a culinary treasure-chest of great produce

from the Basque region. You'll find excellent seasonal fruit and vegetables, breads, delectable cheeses, glistening olives, cured hams and sausages, seafood, wines, ciders and other enticements. **Okamika** (☎943 56 13 28; www.okamika.es; Calle Ipar 1; pintxos €2.50-4.50; ⊙noon-4pm & 7pm-midnight Sun-Tue & Thu, to 2.30am Fri & Sat) is a jewel-box-sized wine and *pintxo* bar, with exposed stone and whitewashed walls, outdoor seating and a great lounge and jazz soundtrack. Stop in for smoked sardines, grilled foie gras with fig jam or grilled scallops with sea urchin roe, matched with a changing selection of by-the-glass wines and over 40 different gins.

Zarautz' **Photomuseum** (www. photomuseum.name; Calle San Ignacio 11; adult/child €6/3, free Wed & Fri; ⊙10am-2pm & 5-8pm Tue-Sun) explores the development of photography and moving pictures. Start up on the 4th floor and work your way downstairs, taking in displays on ombrascopes, magic lanterns and the early cinematic creations of the Lumière brothers. The 1st and 2nd floors are devoted to photography. Don't miss the early 20th-century photographs of the Bilbao artist Luis de Ocharan, who captured fascinating vignettes of Basque rural and urban life in his grainy images.

On a hilltop 3km west of Zarautz overlooking the ocean, winery **Elkano Txakoli** (☎600 800 259; www.txakolielkano.com; Eitzaga Auzoa 24; 1hr tour & tasting €8; ⊙by appointment) has been cultivating vines

Geological Marvels of the Central Coast

Between the Bay of Biscay and the western Pyrenees lies an extraordinary geological treasure, a series of rock layers, built up over time, that offer an astonishing survey of more than 60 million years of life on earth. Running for 13km along the coast, these natural formations known as flysch deposits give a geological record from 50 to 110 million years ago and were formed following the collision of Iberia – once an island – with the continent of Europe. Some geologists believe that a thin black layer embedded in the rocks occurred around 65 million years ago and indicates when an asteroid struck the earth and caused the mass extinction of dinosaurs.

The site, comprising some 89 sq km, is protected as the **Basque Coast Geopark**, and was designated a Unesco Global Geopark in 2015. It spreads across the municipalities of Zumaia, Mutriku and Deba, with marked pathways travelling over the site, though sites of particular geological interest can also be visited on **boat trips** (www.geoparkea.com/en/guided-tours; Muelle Txomin Agirre; ⊘one-hour boat trip adult/child €17/10) departing from Zumaia.

The other great geological attraction of the region is karst, formations made by the eroded limestone of an ancient tropical sea. This slow-acting erosion led to the creation of caves, used by some of the region's earliest humans; places of refuge when the planet turned cold. Their imaginative paintings are preserved in places such as Ekainberri, home to some 70 paintings dating back around 14,000 years – and yet another Unesco World Heritage Site.

The park is set amidst the hilly countryside of the interior, which today is rich Basque farmland. It is bounded to the south by a group of mountains made of Urgonian limestone, which were once barrier reefs. This unusual landscape formed by tectonic deformations is full of paleontological evidence of its marine past, with fossils of bivalves, calcareous plankton and ammonites from the Cretaceous period. Deba and Mutriku are blessed with important archaeological sites, still being studied today.

since 1830, and is now run by the sixth generation. In addition to traditional lightly sparkling white *txakoli*, it also produces a rosé variety. Visits include a vineyard tour and tastings accompanied by snacks such as *gildas* (toothpicks laced with anchovies, olives and peppers).

San Sebastián Neighbourhoods

Central Basque Coast (p89)
Pretty villages and a dramatic coast make this a scenic destination for a road trip. After a seafood meal, bask on a golden beach.

San Sebastián Gros (p141)
Hang on the beach with the surfers, admire the modern architecture of the Kursaal and devote yourself to discovering new culinary horizons.

Hondarribia & Pasaia (p149)
Enjoy superb seafood, stunning sea views, maritime history and verdant peaks in historic Hondarribia and the old port of Pasaia.

San Sebastián Parte Vieja (p103)
This nest of old streets contains the finest pintxo bars in Spain. The aquarium, churches and museum will also appeal.

San Sebastián New Town & Monte Igueldo (p121)
Grandiose and elegant, San Sebastián's new town is perfect for wandering, shopping and enjoying the funfair at Monte Igueldo.

Getaria

San Telmo Museoa

Aquarium

Monte Igueldo

Playa de la Concha

Explore
San Sebastián

From its delightful Old Town, fascinating museums and delicious pintxos restaurants, there are a multitude of reasons why San Sebastián is a tourist favourite. This gorgeous town also has some of Europe's most famous surf beaches on its doorstep.

San Sebastián
Parte Vieja

It only takes a few minutes to stroll the length of San Sebastián's Parte Vieja (Old Quarter), but it might take half a lifetime to sample all the temptations. Every other building seems to house a bar or restaurant, each of which is in intense competition with the others to please the palate.

The Short List

○ **San Telmo Museoa (p104)** *Learning about Basque history at this captivating museum partially set inside a 16th-century convent.*

○ **Monte Urgull (p111)** *Walking up this verdant hill for spectacular beach and city views.*

○ **Aquarium (p106)** *Watching mighty sea creatures glide along inside this excellent aquarium's massive tunnel.*

○ **Basílica de Santa María del Coro (p111)** *Admiring the elaborate facade and altarpiece of San Sebastián's 18th-century baroque beauty.*

○ **Isla de Santa Clara (p113)** *Catching a boat out to this pretty offshore island.*

Getting There & Around

🚶 San Sebastián is small, and with the Parte Vieja sitting pretty much at the centre, it's almost always easier and quicker to walk here from elsewhere.

🚌 Buses linking to other parts of San Sebastián use the bus stops on Alameda del Boulevard.

Neighbourhood Map on p110

San Sebastián's Parte Vieja (Old Quarter) PABKOW/SHUTTERSTOCK ©

Top Experience 📷

Delve into Basque Culture and Society at San Telmo Museoa

Although it's one of the newer museums in the Basque Country, the San Telmo Museoa has actually been around since the 1920s. It was closed for many years, but after major renovation work it reopened in 2011. The displays range from historical artefacts to modern art, with all pieces reflecting Basque culture and society.

◉ MAP P110, D2

📞 943 48 15 80

www.santelmomuseoa.eus

Plaza de Zuloaga 1

adult/child €6/free, Tue free

⊘ 10am-8pm Tue-Sun

The Design

The Basque Country likes to provide its collections with eye-catching homes and the San Telmo Museoa is no exception. The museum has taken a 16th-century Dominican convent with a beautiful cloister and added memorable contemporary architecture, even including a vertical garden.

The Sert Canvases

One of the museum's proudest possessions are the Sert Canvases, located inside the church. The work, created in 1929 by José María Sert, illustrates some of the most important events in San Sebastián's history, including panels on shipbuilding and the sacred oak tree of Gernika.

Memory Traces

Covering the vast period from prehistory to the 19th century, the Memory Traces exhibition delves into Basque origins and the moment in which Basques first looked out to the wider world and set off by boat to explore it.

The Awakening of Modernity

This exhibition covers the great transformations in Basque society that took place during the 19th and 20th centuries, when lifestyles changed from rural to industrial and urban. Exhibits range from traditional farming equipment to 1960s pop culture.

Temporary Exhibitions

The museum prides itself on the broad outlook of its collection, but it's in the frequently changing temporary exhibitions that its diversity becomes truly apparent. These exhibitions might focus one month on mountaineering in the Basque lands and beyond; the following month it could be all about Basque sports.

★ **Top Tips**

○ Labelling is in Spanish and Basque, with free audio guides available in other languages.

○ The connection between pieces can be vague – get a guide (audio or otherwise) to make things clearer.

○ Entry is free on Tuesdays.

○ Spanish- and Basque-language guided tours are offered several times a week; check schedules online.

✗ **Take a Break**

San Telmo Museoa has a small in-house cafe, the **Bokado San Telmo** (☏ 943 57 36 26; www.bokado santelmo.com; Plaza de Zuloaga; pintxos €2-5; ⊙ 10am-8pm Tue, Wed & Sun, 10am-11pm Thu-Sat).

Almost next door to the museum, La Cuchara de San Telmo (p109) serves some of the best *pintxos* in San Sebastián's old town.

Top Experience 📷

Enter an Aquatic Wonderland at Aquarium

Fear for your life as huge sharks bear down behind glass panes, or gaze at otherworldly jellyfish. Highlights of this excellent aquarium include the deep-ocean and coral-reef exhibits, a 12m-long skeleton of a North Atlantic Right Whale, and the long tunnel, around which swim creatures of the deep. Also here is a maritime museum section.

◎ MAP P110, A3

www.aquariumss.com

Plaza Carlos Blasco de Imaz 1

adult/child €13/6.50

⏱10am-9pm Jul & Aug, to 8pm Mon-Fri, to 9pm Sat & Sun Easter-Jun & Sep, to 7pm Mon-Fri, to 8pm Sat & Sun Oct-Easter

Oceanarium & Tunnel

The aquarium's biggest draw for young and old alike is the giant oceanarium tank. It's reached via a see-through tunnel, where you'll see razor-toothed grey nurse (aka sand tiger) sharks, graceful rays, cute turtles, moray eels and various other denizens of the deep. Shark feedings take place at noon on Tuesdays, Thursdays and Saturdays.

Tactile Tank

A favourite with children is the tactile tank, where they can wet their finger tips as they try to handle sea urchins, starfish, blennies, prawns and more. Towards the end of the aquarium is a tank containing slightly transparent shark eggs (dogfish, not great whites) that allow you to see the unborn sharks wriggling about.

Coral Reefs & Mangrove Swamps

Everyone enjoys the oversized tanks of beautiful corals and butterfly-bright tropical marine fish. The 18m-long mangrove swamp display with tree roots reaching into the depths reveals some of the unusual creatures that live in this harsh environment.

Maritime Exhibition

The maritime exhibition takes to the high seas as it explores the Basques' long and adventurous seafaring past and reveals how they were accomplished whalers, in-demand navigators (it was a Basque, Juan Sebastián Elcano, who was the first person to sail around the world) and, controversially, the first Europeans to discover the Americas.

★ **Top Tips**

○ Allow at least 1½ hours for a visit.

○ Last tickets are sold one hour before closing.

○ Try to avoid visiting over Easter and on wet summer days, when crowds can be overwhelming.

○ Audio guides (€2) are worth hiring for more in-depth information.

✕ **Take a Break**

There's no cafe within the aquarium but the surrounding port has a number of decent seafood restaurants, including Restaurante Mariñela (p116).

Perched above the aquarium (and accessed by a lift) is **Bokado Mikel Santamaría** (📞943 43 18 42; www.bokado mikelsantamaria.com; Plaza Jacques Cousteau 1; mains €22-30, tasting menus €54-62; ◷1.30-3.30pm Tue & Sun, 1.30-3.30pm & 9-11pm Wed-Sat), which has memorable views to go with its seafood dishes.

Walking Tour 🥾

Following the Pintxo Trail

There's nothing the people of San Sebastián enjoy more than strolling from bar to bar with friends, sampling one pintxo after another. This walk takes in a selection of the best places to try delicious morsels along with a glass of wine or beer in the atmospheric laneways of the Parte Vieja.

Walk Facts

Start La Mejíllonera
Finish La Viña
Length 800m; two hours

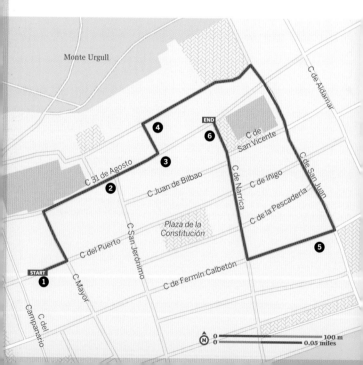

❶ La Mejíllonera

Come to **La Mejíllonera** (📞943 42 84 65; Calle del Puerto 15; mussels €3.90; 🕑6-11pm Mon, 11.30am-3pm & 6-11pm Tue-Thu & Sun, to 11.30pm Fri & Sat) to discover mussels in various glorious forms – including in spicy tomato sauce, with a vinaigrette, in a wine sauce or simply steamed but utterly delectable.

❷ Gandarias

Gandarias (📞943 42 63 62; www. restaurantegandarias.com; Calle 31 de Agosto 23; pintxos €2.50-4.75; 🕑11am-3.30pm & 7pm-midnight) has a sterling reputation for its *pintxos*. Alongside all the classics are house specials such as seared foie gras with redcurrants.

❸ Bar Martinez

Opening its doors in the 1940s, the tiny, character-laden **Bar Martinez** (📞943 42 49 65; www. barmartinezdonosti.com; Calle 31 de Agosto 13; pintxos €2-5.50; 🕑11am-3.30pm & 6.30pm-midnight Sat-Wed, 6.30pm-midnight Fri Jul & Aug, from 7pm Sep-Jun) has had plenty of time to get things right, including the award-winning *morros de bacalao* (slices of cod balanced atop a piece of bread).

❹ La Cuchara de San Telmo

The supremely creative kitchen at **La Cuchara de San Telmo** (📞943 44 16 55; Santa Korda Kalea 4; pintxos €3-5; 🕑7.30-11pm Tue, 12.30-5.30pm & 7.30-11.30pm Wed-Sun) offers miniature *nueva cocina vasca* (Basque nouvelle cuisine). Order delights including slow-roasted suckling pig or veal cheeks in red wine from the blackboard menu behind the counter.

❺ Txalupa Gastroleku

A wooden bar shaped like a *txalupa* (traditional fishing boat), piled high with sublime *pintxos* prepared in the adjoining open kitchen, forms the centrepiece of hotspot **Txalupa Gastroleku** (www.txalupa gastroleku.com; Calle de Fermín Calbetón 3; pintxos €2-5.50; 🕑noon-5pm & 7pm-midnight Mon, 7pm-midnight Wed, noon-5pm & 7pm-2am Thu & Fri, to 3am Sat, to midnight Sun).

❻ La Viña

The bar of **La Viña** (📞943 42 74 95; www.lavinarestaurante.com; Calle 31 de Agosto 3; pintxos €2-3.50, cheesecake €5; 🕑10.30am-5pm & 6.30pm-midnight Tue-Sun) displays a wonderful array of fishy *pintxos* but the real highlight here is the creamy baked cheesecake, cooked daily to a special recipe.

San Sebastián Parte Vieja

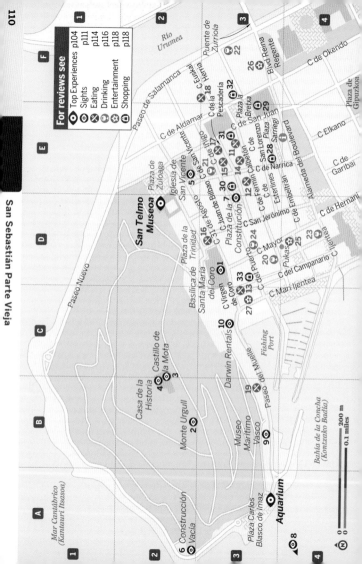

For reviews see
- ◉ Top Experiences p104
- ◎ Sights p111
- ✕ Eating p114
- ◎ Drinking p116
- ◎ Entertainment p118
- ◎ Shopping p118

Mar Cantábrico
(Kantauri Itsasoa)

Río Urumea

Paseo de Salamanca

Plaza de Zuloaga

San Telmo Museoa

Iglesia de San Vicente

Paseo Nuevo

Casa de la Historia

Castillo de la Mota
4 ○ 3

Monte Urgull 2 ◎

Basílica de Santa María del Coro

Plaza de la Trinidad

C 31 de Agosto
16 ✕
5 ◎
C de San Vicente
C de Iñigo
30 ✕ 21 ◎
15 ✕ 17 ✕
11 ◎
14 ✕
C de Fermín
C Juan de Bilbao
Plaza de la Constitución
12 ◎
33 ◎
13 ◎
27 ✕

Museo Marítimo Vasco
9 ◎

Darwin Rentals
19 ✕

Paseo del Muelle

10 ◎
C del Puerto

Fishing Port

C Virgen de Coro
1 ◎

C San Jerónimo
24 ◎
20 ◎
C Mayor
25 ◎
C del Campanario

Puente de Zurriola

26 ✕
Blvd Reina Regente
C de Okendo

Plaza de Gipuzkoa

C de Elkano

C Elkano

C de Garibai

C Euskal Herria
18 ✕
C de Aldamar
C de la Pescadería
32 ◎
C Plaza
C de S Bretxa
29 ◎
C de San Juan
31 ◎
C San Lorenzo
Sarriegi
28 ◎
C de Narrica
C de Embeltrán
C de Hernani
Alameda del Boulevard
C Puka
23 ◎
C Ijentea
C Mari Ijentea

Construcción Vacía 6 ◎

Plaza Carlos Blasco de Imaz

Aquarium ◉

8 ◉◉

Bahía de la Concha
(Kontxako Badia)

200 m
0.1 miles

Sights

Basílica de Santa María del Coro
BASILICA

1  MAP P110, D3

The Parte Vieja's most photogenic building is this baroque basilica, completed in 1774. Its ornate facade depicts St Sebastian and the altarpiece is dedicated to San Sebastián's other patron saint, Our Lady of the Choir. (Basilica of Our Lady of the Choir, Basilica de Nuestra Señora del Coro; Calle 31 de Agosto 46; €3; ⏰10.45am-1.15pm & 4.45-7.45pm)

Monte Urgull
MOUNTAIN

2  MAP P110, B2

You can walk to the summit of Monte Urgull (123m), topped by the low castle walls of the Castillo de la Mota and a grand statue of Christ, by taking a path from Plaza de Zuloaga or from behind the aquarium. The views are breathtaking and the shady parkland on the way up is a peaceful retreat from the city.

Castillo de la Mota
CASTLE

3  MAP P110, C2

At the summit of Monte Urgull, this stone fortress is but the latest incarnation of many fortifications that have existed here since the 12th century. It's well worth huffing your way to the top for the impressive views and the intriguing exhibitions of the Casa de la Historia (p112), located inside the castle walls. (Monte Urgull)

Basílica de Santa María del Coro

The Rise of San Sebastián

It was a queen with bad skin who first put San Sebastián on the international tourist map. In 1845, Queen Isabel II, who suffered from a skin allergy, was advised by her doctor to start bathing in the waters of the southern Bay of Biscay, which have long been known for their therapeutic properties. Her presence each summer attracted the rest of the royal court as well as plenty of aristocrats.

Belle Époque Expansion

The town's increasing popularity brought wealth and development. In 1864 the old city walls were demolished and the new city (Centro Romántico) came into being. During the early part of the 20th century, San Sebastián reached the pinnacle of its fame when Queen Maria Cristina and her court spent the summers here in the Palacio Miramar (p132). It was during this period that the city was given its superb belle époque makeover, which has left it with a legacy of elegant art nouveau buildings and beachfront swagger. Even World War I couldn't put a damper on the party – the city was used by the European elite as a retreat from the war raging elsewhere.

Re-Emergence

The good times didn't last, however. The combined effects of the Spanish Civil War followed by World War II finally put out the lights, and for decades the city languished until the tide again turned in San Sebastián's favour. In the latter half of the 20th century, the city underwent a major revival. Its overall style and excitement give it a growing reputation as an important venue for international cultural and commercial events. The beachfront area now contains some of the most expensive properties in Spain and the city is firmly entrenched on the Spanish tourist trail, which gives it a highly international feel. In 2016, it was designated European Capital of Culture, a title it shared with the Polish city of Wrocław.

Casa de la Historia MUSEUM

4 ◎ MAP P110, B2

Inside the grounds of the Castillo de la Mota (p111) is this small museum focusing on the city's history. It has audiovisual exhibits that touch on San Sebastián's traditional festivals, historical artefacts from days past (including military uniforms used in the Carlist Wars), and photographs and models showing the city's evolution over the years. (www.santelmomuseoa.eus; Monte Urgull; admission free; ⏱11am-8pm Jul & Aug,

10am-5.30pm Wed-Sun Easter-Jun & Sep-Nov)

Iglesia de San Vicente CHURCH

5 ◉ MAP P110, E2

Lording it over the Parte Vieja, this striking church is thought to be the oldest building in San Sebastián. Its origins date to the 12th century, but it was rebuilt in its current Gothic form in the early 1500s. The towering facade gives onto an echoing vaulted interior, featuring an elaborate gold altarpiece and a 19th-century French organ. Also impressive are the stained-glass rose windows. (Calle de San Vicente 3; ◷9am-1pm & 5-8pm)

Construcción Vacía SCULPTURE

6 ◉ MAP P110, A2

At the base of Monte Urgull is Jorge Oteiza's *Construcción Vacía (Empty Space)* sculpture. Oteiza (1908–2003) was a renowned painter, sculptor and writer who was born and brought up close to San Sebastián. An award winner at the 1957 São Paulo Biennale, the rust-red work looks best on a dark and stormy day or at sunset. (Paseo Nuevo)

Plaza de la Constitución SQUARE

7 ◉ MAP P110, D3

One of the Basque Country's most attractive city squares, the Plaza de la Constitución was built in 1813 at the heart of the old town on the site of an older square. It was once used as a bullring; the balconies of the fringing houses were rented to spectators.

Isla de Santa Clara ISLAND

8 ◉ MAP P110, A4

Lying 750m offshore from Playa de la Concha, this little island is accessible by **Motoras de la Isla** (☏943 00 04 50; www.motorasde laisla.com; Lasta Plaza; return trip standard boat €4, glass-bottom boat €6.50; ◷10am-8pm Jun-Sep) boats that run every half-hour from the fishing port in the summer. At low tide the island gains its own tiny beach and you can climb its forested paths to a small lighthouse. There are also picnic tables and a summertime kiosk.

Museo Marítimo Vasco MUSEUM

9 ◉ MAP P110, B3

This museum turns the pages of Basque seafaring and naval history. There is no permanent collection, just long-term exhibitions, which in the past have featured themes of whaling, shipwrecks, women and the sea, and the Basque coastline in art. While there usually isn't much English-language signage, English brochures are available. (Euskal Itsas Museoa; ☏943 43 00 51; www. itsasmuseoa.eus; Paseo del Muelle 24; admission free; ◷10am-2pm & 4-7pm Tue-Sat, from 11am Sun mid-Jun–mid-Sep, closed Sun afternoon mid-Sep–mid-Jun)

Post-Lunch Planning

Make sure you have a plan for after-lunch activities, as most shops close for a long siesta. It's a perfect time to head to the beach for a bit of seaside relaxation.

Darwin Rentals

WATER SPORTS

10 🎯 MAP P110, C3

On the harbourfront, Darwin Rentals hires out state-of-the-art inflatable two-person kayaks, SUPs (stand-up paddleboards) and skimboards, as well as electric scooters and motorised skateboards. Friendly staff provide great insider tips on the best locations to use the equipment. (📞 637 853811; www.darwinrentals.es; Paseo del Muelle 1; equipment hire per 2/4/12 hours €15/30/60; 🕙 10am-10pm May-Oct)

Eating

Bodegón Alejandro

BASQUE €€€

11 🍴 MAP P110, E3

Tucked down the steps off a pedestrian-packed street, this handsome cellar restaurant is acclaimed for its Basque cooking. The small, changing menu has succulent treats such as local Idiazabal cheese soufflé, spider crab salad with fennel cream, crispy-skin hake with a zesty lemon vinaigrette, and roast quail with red wine jus. (📞 943 42 71 58; www.bodegonalejandro.com; Calle de Fermín Calbetón 4; mains €21-24; 🕙 1-3.30pm & 8.30-10.30pm Jun–mid-Oct, 1-3.30pm Tue & Sun, 1-3.30pm & 8.30-10.30pm Wed-Sat mid-Oct–May)

Casa Urola

PINTXOS €

12 🍴 MAP P110, E3

Founded in 1956, Casa Urola has hefty stone walls, hams hanging above the bar and a blackboard menu chalking up the day's *pintxos*. Join the lunch and evening crowds flocking for perfectly turned-out bites, such as grilled white asparagus, foie gras with pear compote, hake tacos, and mushroom and Idiazabal cheese tart. (📞 943 44 13 71; www.casaurolajatetxea.es; Calle de Fermín Calbetón 20; pintxos €2-4; 🕙 noon-3pm & 7-11pm Wed-Mon)

Restaurante Kokotxa

GASTRONOMY €€€

13 🍴 MAP P110, C3

Hidden in an overlooked Parte Vieja alley, this Michelin-starred restaurant rewards those who search. Most people opt for the *menú de mercado* and enjoy the flavours of the busy city market. Note that there are just 30 seats, making advance reservations essential, and that no-choice menus mean dietary restrictions can't be accommodated. (📞 943 42 19 04; www.restaurantekokotxa.com; Calle del Campanario 11; 9-/14-course menus €88/120; 🕙 1.30-3pm & 8.30-10.30pm

Tue–Sat, closed late Feb–mid-Mar, 1st week Jun & last 2 weeks Oct)

Bar Borda Berri

PINTXOS €

14 ✖ MAP P110, E3

Perennially popular Bar Borda Berri is an old-school *pintxo* bar – with black-and-white chequerboard floors and mustard-coloured walls hung with old photos and strands of garlic – that really lives up to the hype. Hungry diners crowd in for house specials such as braised veal cheeks in wine, mushroom and Idiazabal sheep's cheese risotto, and beef-rib skewers. (☎ 943 43 03 42; Calle de Fermín Calbetón 12; pintxos €2-4; ⊘ 12.30-3.30pm & 7.30-11pm Wed-Sat, 12.30-3.30pm Sun Sep-Jun, also Mon & Tue Jul & Aug.)

Txepetxa

PINTXOS €

15 ✖ MAP P110, E3

The humble *antxoa* (anchovy) is elevated to royal status at this old-fashioned, wood-panelled local favourite. You can order it in over a dozen different ways, topped with everything from salmon roe to spider crab mayonnaise. (☎ 943 42 22 27; www.facebook.com/bartxepetxa; Calle de la Pescadería 5; pintxos €2-3.50; ⊘ 7-11pm Tue, noon-3pm & 7-11pm Wed-Sun)

Txuleta

PINTXOS €€

16 ✖ MAP P110, D3

A *txuleta* is a cut of beef and this is the place to sample some wonderful melt-in-your mouth examples – try the *pintxo txuleta*, a mini kebab of three bite-sized

Iglesia de San Vicente (p113)

chunks of tender beef, or *solomillo al Oporto* (crusty bread topped with sirloin with port sauce). Its restaurant serves a full menu of steaks as well as seafood. (☎943 44 10 07; www.txuletarestaurante.com; Plaza de la Trinidad 2; pintxos €2-4.50, mains €13.50-24; ⏱noon-4pm Mon, noon-4pm & 7-11.30pm Wed-Sun)

Bar Nestor
BASQUE €€

17 ✕ MAP P110, E3

Wonderfully eccentric Bar Nestor has a cult following for its tortillas made with green peppers (just one tortilla is cooked at lunch and at dinner; put your name on the list for a portion – in person only – an hour prior to service), and its steaks (advance reservations are possible by phone, otherwise arrive early as seating is limited). (☎943 42 48 73; www.facebook.com/barnestorss; Calle de la Pescadería 11; tortilla €2.20, steak per kilo €44; ⏱1-3pm & 8-11pm Tue-Sat, 1-3pm Sun)

Astelena
BASQUE €€€

18 ✕ MAP P110, F3

With a whitewashed main dining room and stone-walled cellar, this is a classy place to linger over beautifully prepared seafood and roast meat dishes. Highlights include chargrilled squid with caramelised onions, smoked duck breast with burnt-orange marmalade, and rice with octopus and clams. (☎943 42 58 67; www.restauranteastelena.com; Calle

Euskal Herria 3; mains €18.50-26, tasting menu €50; ⏱1.30-3pm & 8.30-10.30pm Tue & Thu-Sat, 1.30-3pm Wed & Sun)

Restaurante Mariñela
SEAFOOD €€

19 ✕ MAP P110, B3

Set with checked tablecloths and outdoor tables on the cobblestones facing the harbourfront, this casual spot does delicious simply grilled fish and seafood plates. Go early to beat the crowds. As a plan B there are several similar neighbouring places. (☎943 42 13 88; www.marinela-igeldo.com; Paseo del Muelle; mains €14-24, seafood platter €88; ⏱noon-11pm Jul & Aug, noon-3.45pm & 7-10.30pm Mar-Jun, Sep & Oct)

Drinking

Côte Bar
COCKTAIL BAR

20 🍷 MAP P110, D3

Once the *pintxo* bars have battened down the hatches for the night, search out this low-key cocktail bar to see in the small hours. It's a stylish place, with a black granite bar and red, orange and yellow lighting, where you can sip on classic cocktails and superlative G&Ts. (www.facebook.com/cotebardonostia; Calle de Fermín Calbertón 48; ⏱5pm-3am Mon-Thu, to 4.30am Fri & Sat, 4pm-3am Sun; 🛜)

The Day the Duke Came to Visit

You might think that Calle 31 de Agosto, at the northern end of the Parte Vieja, is named after the glorious days of late summer. But not quite. The road name actually commemorates one of the darker days in San Sebastián's history. On 31 August 1813, the Duke of Wellington's Anglo-Portuguese army captured the city from the French during the Napoleonic Wars, ransacked it and then burnt it down. Only a handful of houses and the churches of San Vicente (p113) and the Basílica de Santa María del Coro (p111) survived. To make matters worse, the Spanish and British were supposed to be on the same side. Today, candles are lit on the balconies lining this street every 31 August to recall the dreadful day.

Garua

CRAFT BEER

21 🚇 MAP P110, E3

Fitted out with timber panels and exposed brick, this tri-level bar has seven Basque craft beers on the taps at any one time. Breweries represented include San Sebastián's Basqueland and Bilbao's Bidassoa; there are also bottled Basque, Spanish and international craft beers, *txakoli*, Basque spirits and liqueurs. (Calle de Iñigo 5; ⏰6pm-midnight Tue-Thu, to 1am Fri, 1pm-1am Sat, 1-11pm Sun)

Be Club

CLUB

22 🚇 MAP P110, F3

Hosting DJs throughout the week and live gigs ranging from soul and funk to Afrobeat, hip-hop and acid jazz most weekends, this cool little late-night club has an extensive gin collection, craft beers and seasonally inspired cocktails. (www.beclubss.com; Paseo de Salamanca 3; ⏰3pm-5am Sun-Thu, to 6.30am Fri & Sat)

Dioni's

BAR

23 🚇 MAP P110, D4

Great for a drink on its sunny terrace or a DJ-fuelled party on Friday and Saturday nights, Dioni's has a glam 1980s cocktail-bar ambience. (www.facebook.com/bardionis; Calle Ijentea 2; ⏰3pm-2.30am Mon-Thu & Sun, to 3.30am Fri & Sat; 🛜)

Arkaitzpe

BAR

24 🚇 MAP P110, D3

DJs spin funk and Latino beats most nights (nightly in summer) in this old-town bar's basement. Cocktails inspired by Latin America (mojitos, caipirinhas, pisco sours, daiquiris et al) pack a punch; it also has strong sangria. Arrive early in summer, when queues form outside the door. (www.arkaitzpe.es; Calle Mayor 14; ⏰3pm-3am Sun-Thu, to 4.30am Fri & Sat)

San Sebastián's Surf Icon

Pukas (Map p110, D4; 📞943 42 72 28; www.pukassurf.com; Calle Mayor 5; ⏲10am-8.30pm Mon-Fri, 10.30am-9pm Sat) is a historic name in San Sebastián's surfing circles, running a surf school near Gros' Zurriola beach and a number of shops across town, including this one in the Parte Vieja. As well as an array of boards, you can browse the full range of beach fashions, from bikinis and sunglasses to trainers, caps and T-shirts.

Entertainment

Teatro Principal   THEATRE

25 ⭐ MAP P110, D4

San Sebastián's oldest theatre dates back to 1843, although it has been reconstructed over the years. Today, the 576-seat hall hosts a packed calendar of theatre and dance performances. (📞943 48 19 70; www.donostiakultura.eus; Calle Mayor 3)

Altxerri Jazz Bar   LIVE MUSIC

26 ⭐ MAP P110, F3

This jazz-and-blues temple has regular live gigs by local and international artists. Arrive early to get a seat and enjoy a cocktail while you wait; music generally starts around 8.30pm to 9pm. Jam sessions take over on nights with no gig; there's also an in-house art gallery that fosters the work of young contemporary artists. (www. altxerri.com; Blvd Reina Regente 2; ⏲7pm-2.30am Sun-Thu, to 3.30am Fri & Sat)

Etxekalte   JAZZ

27 ⭐ MAP P110, C3

Near the harbour, this late-night haunt set over two floors hosts live jazz and blues, plus other genres such as traditional Basque music, and often has DJs. (www.facebook. com/etxekaltejazzclub; Calle Mari 11; ⏲6pm-4am Tue-Thu & Sun, 6pm-5am Fri & Sat)

Shopping

Casa Ponsol   HATS

28 🔒 MAP P110, E3

In business since 1838, this hat shop evokes the elegance of a bygone era. The bright and sunny interior has lots of great styles for men and women with international brands such as Stetson, Kangol and Crambes, as well as authentic Panama hats and Casa Ponsol's own berets. (📞943 42 08 76; www. casaponsol.com; Calle de Narrica 4; ⏲10am-1pm & 4-8pm Mon-Fri, to 1.30pm & 4-8pm Sat)

Mercado de la Bretxa   MARKET

29 🔒 MAP P110, E3

Dating to 1870, San Sebastián's Mercado de la Bretxa is now home to chain stores, but adjacent to it, accessed via escalators in a glass kiosk-like building, is the underground covered market where every chef in the old town comes to get the freshest produce. It's an ideal place to stock up on picnic supplies. (Plaza la Bretxa; ⏱8am-9pm Mon-Sat)

Alboka Artesanía   ARTS & CRAFTS

30 🔒 MAP P110, E3

Crafts and objects made in the Basque Country fill this shop on one of the old town's prettiest plazas. You'll find ceramics, tea towels, marionettes, picture frames, T-shirts, pelota balls and of course those iconic oversized berets. (Plaza de la Constitución; ⏱10.30am-1.30pm & 4-8pm Mon-Fri, 10.30am-8.30pm Sat, 11am-2.30pm Sun)

Beltza   MUSIC

31 🔒 MAP P110, E3

Browse for vinyl and CDs from the Basque Country and beyond at this chequerboard-tiled record shop. Cash only. (www.beltzarecords.com; Calle de San Juan 9; ⏱11am-1.30pm & 4-8pm Mon-Sat)

Aitor Lasa   FOOD & DRINKS

32 🔒 MAP P110, F3

This high-quality deli is the place to stock up on ingredients for a gourmet picnic, with a heavenly array of cheeses, mushrooms and seasonal fruit and vegetables. (www.aitorlasa.com; Calle de Aldamar 12; ⏱8.30am-2pm & 5-8pm Mon-Fri, 8.30am-2.30pm Sat)

Room 278   GIFTS & SOUVENIRS

33 🔒 MAP P110, D3

Though small in size, Room 278 has loads of great gift ideas, including prints of picturesque San Sebastián scenes, rugged canvas bags, mugs, pillowcases, cushions, tea towels and more. (www.room278shop.com; Calle del Puerto 24; ⏱12.30-5.30pm Mon-Sat, 11am-6pm Sun)

Explore ⊚

San Sebastián New Town & Monte Igueldo

A scenic area for strolling, San Sebastián's elegant new town, or Centro Romántico, has wide, straight streets lined by stately belle époque buildings and glamorous boutiques. Further west is the upmarket seaside neighbourhood of Ondarreta and fun-filled Monte Igueldo.

The Short List

○ **Playa de la Concha (p122)** *Lazing away the day at this lovely protected beach.*

○ **Monte Igueldo (p124)** *Riding the funicular railway up to the funfair-topped hill with magnificent views over the seaside city.*

○ **Catedral del Buen Pastor de San Sebastián (p131)** *Visiting the new town's soaring 19th-century cathedral.*

○ **Teatro Victoria Eugenia (p136)** *Taking in a performance at the city's beautiful belle époque theatre.*

○ **Puente de Maria Cristina (p131)** *Crossing the Río Urumea along this resplendent bridge.*

Getting There & Around

🚶 The best way to explore is on foot. From the heart of Parte Vieja it's about a 15-minute walk to Playa de la Concha's centre.

🚌 Bus 16 travels from the centre to the base of Monte Igueldo via Playa de la Concha.

Neighbourhood Map on p128

Top Experience 📷
Hit the Beach at Playa de la Concha

Fulfilling almost every idea of what a perfect city beach should be like, Playa de la Concha is framed by the Parte Vieja, beautiful parks and flowery belle époque ('beautiful era') buildings. Tanned and toned bodies spread across the sand throughout the long summer months, when a fiesta atmosphere prevails. Its sheltered position means the swimming is almost always safe.

◎ MAP P128, E4

Paseo de la Concha

The Beach

Playa de la Concha is a wide half-moon-shaped bay of soft sand, lapping waves, stunning views and a buzzing beach scene.

Tides vary enormously here; when it's high, the beach's width can be as little as 40m, so make sure your possessions don't get washed away.

Paseo de la Concha

The promenade that curves along the 1.3km-long beach, Paseo de la Concha, makes for a lovely stroll. Lined by an ornamental wrought iron balustrade, it's a favourite with joggers and strollers, particularly in the early evening when everyone turns out to enjoy the bracing sea air and soft summer light. After dark, it's illuminated by belle époque lampposts, with magical views of the city's twinkling lights reflecting in the lapping water.

Historic Buildings

Overlooking the west side of the beach, the Palacio Miramar (p132) was the summer villa of Maria Cristina, a beach-loving 19th-century royal. Further around, La Perla spa and restaurant complex is a local landmark, an ornate 1912 pavilion that was once the royal bathing house. Its saltwater spas can now be enjoyed by everyone at the Perla Thalasso Sports Centre (p132).

Beachfront Partying

The Playa is home to a number of cafes and nightlife hotspots, such as Café de la Concha (p133). For late night dancing, the historic Bataplan Disco (p134) overlooking the sand is the place to go.

★ Top Tips

o The swim out to Isla de Santa Clara (p113) is tempting, but it's further than it looks. Paddle from Playa de Ondarreta (p130) instead: it's closer and there are summertime rest platforms on the way.

o Playa de la Concha rarely has surf, but even so, obey the summer lifeguards, because conditions change fast. For waves, head to nearby Playa de la Zurriola (p143) in Gros.

o Parking close to the beach is very difficult (if not impossible) at peak times.

✕ Take a Break

There are lots of places to grab a snack or an ice cream around the beach; for the latter, try Arnoldo Heladería (p132).

Built into the pavilions that back the beach is the art deco Café de la Concha (p133), which has all-day dining and out-of-this-world views.

Top Experience 📷
Enjoy Mountain-top Views at Monte Igueldo

At the far western end of the Bahía de la Concha is the fun-filled Monte Igueldo. Attractions include a funicular railway to the summit and a funfair. While this might sound like child's play, the views from the top are like nectar to lovers of sunsets. Clifftop coastal walks also provide inspiration for hikers to make the trip.

⊙ MAP P128, A3

www.monteigueldo.es

€2.30

🕐 10am-9pm Mon-Fri, to 10pm Sat & Sun Jul, to 10pm Aug, to 8pm Mon-Fri, to 9pm Sat & Sun Jun & Sep, shorter hours Oct-May

Funicular Railway

The **funicular railway** (www.monteigueldo.es; Plaza del Funicular; return adult/child €3.75/2.50; ⏱10am-10pm Jun-Aug, shorter hours Sep-May) has been clattering up the side of Monte Igueldo since 1912, allowing you to enjoy old-world transport. It's the best option for accessing the glorious views from the top of the hill. It departs every 15 minutes.

The Views

The views from the summit of Monte Igueldo will make you feel like a circling hawk staring over the vast panorama of the Bahía de la Concha and the surrounding coastline and mountains.

Parque de Atracciones

At the **funfair** (☎943 21 35 25; www.monteigueldo. es; Paseo de Igeldo; ⏱11am-11.30pm Aug, hours vary Feb-Jul & Sep-Dec) atop Monte Igueldo, individual attractions include roller coasters, boat rides and carousels. Each ride costs between €1 and €5. Opening hours fluctuate throughout the year and the park closes in January; check the website for schedules.

Sunset

When the weather gods are smiling, Monte Igueldo is a fine place to be at sunset: watch as the orange sun drops into the ocean and the lighthouse adds its own light show.

Torreón de Monte Igueldo

The striking **Tower of Monte Igueldo** (www. monteigueldo.es/the-tower; Monte Igueldo; adult/ child €2.50/1.50) is a fortified 16th-century lighthouse. It no longer works (there's a new lighthouse nearby), but it offers a great vantage point.

★ **Top Tips**

○ The sweeping views from 181m-high Monte Igueldo over the Bahía de La Concha and Parte Vieja are worth the trip alone.

○ Weekends, when local families come with children, might be the busiest times to visit, but are also the most festive.

○ While there is a car park at the top, spaces are limited; it's easier to take the funicular.

✕ **Take a Break**

There are various cheap and cheerful snack bars at the top of Monte Igueldo.

Directly below Monte Igueldo, footsteps from the funicular in the San Sebastián Royal Tennis Club, Restaurante Tenis Ondarreta (p133) has inventive Basque cuisine and an adjacent English pub.

Walking Tour 🚶🚶

Old & New in San Sebastián

Small, compact and very pedestrian-friendly, San Sebastián lends itself to gentle ambles. In the space of a few hundred metres you can pass by crowded pintxo bars, pretty churches, a couple of outrageously beautiful urban beaches, tempting designer clothes shops and some elegant bridges. This circular walk takes you through the best of the city centre.

Walk Facts

Start/Finish Parque de Alderdi Eder

Length 3.5km; three hours

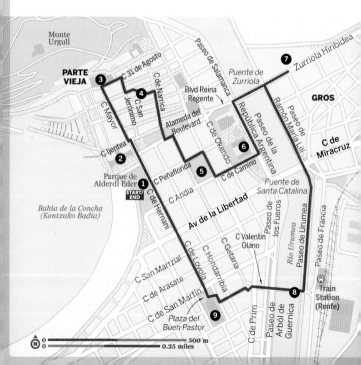

❶ Parque de Alderdi Eder

Overlooking the magnificent Playa de la Concha, the Parque de Alderdi Eder (p131) is a real city social centre. It's not so much of a grassy park as it is a formally laid out plaza, but there are lots of trees and plenty going on.

❷ Ayuntamiento

Once a casino, the Ayuntamiento (p132) is one of the most impressive buildings in San Sebastián, even if what goes on inside the city's town hall is less glamorous today (but probably just as full of intrigue!).

❸ Basílica de Santa María del Coro

The intimate and artistic Basílica de Santa María del Coro (p111) is the Parte Vieja's best-loved church.

❹ Plaza de la Constitución

San Sebastián's most photogenic plaza, the Parte Vieja's Plaza de la Constitución (p113) once hosted bullfights. Today it's ringed by *pintxo* bars spilling onto outdoor terraces.

❺ Plaza de Gipuzkoa

It might be called a plaza, but with its duck-filled pond, flowerbeds and many trees, the 19th-century Plaza de Gipuzkoa (p130) is as much a formal garden park as a city square.

❻ Hotel Maria Cristina

Peek inside the lobby of the early 20th-century Hotel Maria Cristina (p130), whose first guest was the namesake regent of Spain. Today, the hotel is still one of the city's grandest, and is a riverside landmark.

❼ Kursaal

Cross the river via the Puente de Zurriola bridge to Gros and admire the Kursaal (p146) building, the city's modernist wonder. Opened in 1999, its design is said to represent two beached rocks. Head around the back to check the surf on Playa de la Zurriola.

❽ Puente de Maria Cristina

Follow the river upstream along the Gros side to the prettiest bridge in the city, the Puente de Maria Cristina (p131). It's a belle époque creation most notable for its golden statues of winged angels atop rearing horses.

❾ Catedral del Buen Pastor de San Sebastián

From the Puente de Maria Cristina, on the new town side of the river, make your way to the city's magnificent Catedral del Buen Pastor de San Sebastián (p131), which was consecrated in 1897. Its stained-glass windows depict the 12 apostles.

A **B** **C** **D**

1

Mar Cantábrico
(Kantauri Itsasoa)

Isla de
Santa Clara

Parque
Igueldo

Punta
Torrepea

2 ● Peine del Viento

Paseo del Faro

Monte Igueldo

3 ◉ 🟡 17 ✕ ← Paseo de
Eduardo Chillida

*Plaza del
Funicular*

Bahía de la Concha
(Kontxako Badia)

3

4

ONDARRETA

C de Brunet

C de Pamplona

C de Vitoria-
Gasteiz

Av de Satrústegui

2 ◉ Playa de
Ondarreta

Pico del
Loro

9 ◉

Paseo de la Concha

Paseo de Miraconcha

Plaza de
Alfonso XIII

3 ◉ Palacio
Miramar

Jardines de
Miramar

27 🔒

C de Matia

C Erregezain

ANTIGUO

29 ✪

5

For reviews see

◉	Top Experiences	p122
◉	Sights	p130
✕	Eating	p132
🟡	Drinking	p134
✪	Entertainment	p136
🔒	Shopping	p137

6

0 ——— 500 m
0 ——— 0.25 miles

A **B** **C** **D**

E

F

PARTE VIEJA

GROS 1

Paseo del Muelle

Fishing Port

Puente de Zurriola

C de Aldamar

C de San Juan

C Mayor

C Marijenea

Alameda del Boulevard

Blvd Reina Regente

Paseo de Salamanca

Paseo de la República Argentina

Paseo de Ramón María Lili

Puente de Santa Catalina 2

Ayuntamiento

21

10

30

12

C Elkano

34

C de Okendo

26

23

28

4

Hotel María Cristina

C sta Catalina

Parque de Alderdi Eder

6

C de Hernani

C Peñaflorida

C de Garibai

Plaza de Gipuzkoa

5

16

C Andia

31

11

33

C Etxaide

C Bergara

Av de la Libertad

Plaza de Cervantes

C de Loyola

C Hondarribia

C Getaria

Paseo de los Fueros

Río Urumea

Train Station (Renfe) 3

15

35

C de Urbieta

32

C de Arrasate

C de San Martín

C Valentín Olano

8

25

Puente de María Cristina

Catedral del Buen Pastor de San Sebastián

7

Plaza del Buen Pastor

C de Urdaneta

Paseo de la Concha

C de Zubieta

C de Mantería

C del Triunfo

C de la Marina

13

Playa de la Concha

14

19

36

1

20

22

C de Prim

C de los Reyes Católicos

La Perla Thalasso Sports Centre

C San Bartolomé

CENTRO ROMÁNTICO

Koldo Mitxelena Kulturunea

18

24

C de Larramendi

C de Moraza

C de Arbol de Guernica

4

Cuesta de Aldapeta

Parque Basoerdi

Amara Train Station (ET/FV)

C de Easo

C de Egana

5

6

E

F

G

H

Sights

Koldo Mitxelena Kulturunea

CULTURAL CENTRE

1 ⊙ MAP P128, G4

Set in a grand neoclassical building dating from the 1890s, this cultural centre has a packed line-up of art exhibitions, book launches, discussions and more. Don't miss the galleries downstairs, which mount free, thought-provoking exhibitions. The centre is named after Koldo Mitxelena, a writer and linguist, and one of the great champions of creating a unified Basque language. (☎943 11 27 60; http://kmk.gipuzkoakultura.eus; Calle de Urdaneta 9; admission free; ⏰11am-2pm & 4-8pm Tue-Sat)

Playa de Ondarreta

BEACH

2 ⊙ MAP P128, B4

Playa de Ondarreta, the western extension of the renowned Playa de la Concha, has a less glam, more genteel atmosphere. It's long been popular with the city's most wealthy visitors and residents (look for the former royal summer palace of Miramar that overlooks the beach). Blue-and-white-striped canvas beach cabanas and volleyball nets dot the sands.

Jardines de Miramar

PARK

3 ⊙ MAP P128, B4

Overlooking Playa de la Concha and Playa de Ondarreta, the grassy lawns of the Jardines de Miramar slope gently down to the ocean and are a popular place to catch some sun for those who don't like to get sand between their toes. (Paseo de la Concha; ⏰8am-9pm Apr-Sep, to 7pm Oct-Mar)

Hotel Maria Cristina

HISTORIC BUILDING

4 ⊙ MAP P128, H2

A wonderful example of belle époque architecture, the Hotel Maria Cristina was designed by Charles Mewes, the architect responsible for the Ritz hotels in Paris and London. It first opened its doors in 1912; the first guest was the regent of Spain, Maria Cristina. Today, anyone can enter the lobby and admire the understated luxury, or browse the items on sale at the Mimo San Sebastián Gourmet Shop (p138). (☎943 43 76 00; www.hotel-mariacristina.com; Paseo de la República Argentina 4)

Plaza de Gipuzkoa

PARK

5 ⊙ MAP P128, G2

Designed in 1877 by French landscape artist Pierre Ducasse, who also created the Jardines de Miramar, this little park is one of San Sebastián's loveliest oases, with a duck pond, a small stream crossed by a little footbridge, and a waterfall. A small temple-like structure shelters a meteorological barometer and planetary chart; also here are two large clocks (one made of flowers) and a statue of pianist and composer José María Usandizaga.

Parque de Alderdi Eder PARK

6 ◉ MAP P128, F2

One of the most attractive and enjoyable little outdoor spaces in San Sebastián, the Parque de Alderdi Eder is actually more of an elongated plaza shaded by trees, dotted with benches and busy with children and families enjoying the old-fashioned carousel and numerous street performers. Brilliant views unfold over Playa de la Concha. (Calle de Hernani)

Catedral del Buen Pastor de San Sebastián CATHEDRAL

7 ◉ MAP P128, G3

The dominant building of the new town is the city cathedral, overlooking a busy plaza. Built from slate and sandstone quarried from Monte Igueldo, the cathedral was consecrated in 1897 and has a 75m-high bell tower. Under the foundation stone of the cathedral is a lead box containing pictures of the Spanish royal family and the pope at the time of construction. (Plaza del Buen Pastor; ⏲8am-noon & 5-8pm)

Puente de Maria Cristina BRIDGE

8 ◉ MAP P128, H3

Several bridges span the narrow Río Urumea, but by far the most impressive is the Puente de Maria Cristina. Opened in 1905, the belle époque structure is most notable for its four golden-statue-crowned obelisks, two of which guard the entrance on each side.

Peine del Viento by Eduardo Chillida (p134)

Palacio Miramar

PALACE

9 ◎ MAP P128, C4

When a royal family comes to the seaside, they need a suitable summer beach pad. For Maria Cristina and family, that was the Palacio Miramar. It was built in the late 19th century in a 'Queen Anne English cottage' style (some cottage!), but sadly the interior is closed to the public. (Paseo de la Concha)

Historic Spa

Halfway along the beachfront is the unmistakable white confection of the **Perla Thalasso Sports Centre** (Map p128, E4; ☑943 45 88 56; www.laperla.net; Paseo la Concha; 2/3hr session €29.50/33.50; ◎8am-10pm), a highly rated spa that offers a comprehensive set of treatments inside a grand 1912 building dating from the belle époque ('beautiful era' in French, between the end of the Franco-Prussian War in 1871 and outbreak of WWI in 1914).

The complex features various pools, a sauna, relaxation room, and a Jacuzzi with panoramic views. As with other thalassotherapy centres, La Perla uses seawater in all its aquatic facilities. There's also a gym with group classes (aquafitness, core building, cycling) and a lovely terrace cafe with a full menu.

Ayuntamiento

HISTORIC BUILDING

10 ◎ MAP P128, F2

San Sebastián's town hall is an impressive configuration of belle époque towers and domed ceilings that stands proudly at the meeting point between Playa de la Concha, the Centro Romántico and the Parte Vieja. It began life as the Gran Casino in 1887, before becoming the town hall in 1947. (Town Hall; Parque de Alderdi Eder)

Eating

Antonio Bar

BASQUE €€

11 🍴 MAP P128, G2

From the outside, Antonio Bar looks like the sort of cafe you'd get in a train station waiting room. Hidden downstairs, however, is its six-table basement dining room, where house-speciality stews include *marmitako de bonito* (bonito, potato, red pepper and tomato) and *callos y morros* (beef tripe, blood sausage and chickpeas). *Pintxos* are served at the bar. (☑943 42 98 15; www.antoniobar.com; Calle de Vergara 3; pintxos €2-4.50, mains €17-24; ◎1-3.30pm & 7-11pm Mon-Sat)

Arnoldo Heladeria

ICE CREAM €

12 🍴 MAP P128, F2

In business since 1935, Arnoldo Heladeria makes San Sebastián's best ice cream. Alongside sorbets such as mango and passion fruit, and white peach, they make richer, creamier varieties like sherry-soaked raisin, salted walnut and chocolate-raspberry, plus ice lollies, milk shakes and frappés. From July to September, you can place orders over €12.50 by phone and collect them at beach pick-up points. (☏654 320097; www.arnoldoheladeria.com; Calle de Garibai 2; ice cream per 1/2 scoops €2.30/3; ☽8am-11pm Mon-Thu, to 1am Fri-Sun)

Altuna
PINTXOS €

13 🍴 MAP P128, F4

Decorated in jade-green tiles, this contemporary stunner serves freshly shucked oysters and inventive *pintxos*, such as dried tuna and cold almond soup served in a shot glass, and smoked prickly pear with *jamón* and orange dust. (☏943 57 53 56; www.facebook.com/altunabar; Calle de San Martín 43; pintxos €2.50-4.50, 3 oysters €7-8.50; ☽7-11pm Mon, noon-4pm & 7-11pm Tue-Sat)

Café de la Concha
BASQUE €€

14 🍴 MAP P128, E4

The Café de la Concha is inside a wonderful art deco building that recalls San Sebastián's aristocratic heyday. As regal as the history are the views – you're almost sitting among the sunbathers on the beach. Alongside beach cafe fare (breakfasts, salads, burgers...) are more gourmet mains such as truffle potato gratin, tuna tataki with tomato jam or 12-hour-cooked lamb confit. (☏943 47 36 00; www.cafedelaconcha.com; Paseo de la Concha 10; mains €13-20; ☽9am-midnight; 🛜)

Rojo y Negro
PINTXOS €

15 🍴 MAP P128, F3

You can eat a full sit-down meal at this bar, but you're best following the locals' lead and concentrating on *pintxos* such as cuttlefish miniburgers, crispy pig's ears, grilled foie gras with apricot purée and crab baked in its shell, washed down with a *txakoli* sangria.
For breakfast try the *tosta a la catalana:* toast, tomato, olive oil and garlic. (☏943 35 83 82; www.rojoynegrodonosti.es; Calle San Marcial 52; pintxos €3-4.50, mains €8.50-16; ☽7am-1am Mon-Thu, 7am-2am Fri & Sat, 8am-1am Sun)

Kata 4
SEAFOOD €€

16 🍴 MAP P128, H2

An urbane crowd gather at this fashionable spot near the ritzy Hotel Maria Cristina to feast on eight different varieties of oysters and refined *pintxos*, such as tempura soft-shell crab or ham-wrapped scallops with blood orange butter. Seafood standouts on its restaurant menu include grilled grouper with seaweed emulsion and a corn financier, and truffled pan-fried clams. (☏943 42 32 43; www.kata4.com; Calle Santa Catalina 4; pintxos & oysters €2-4, mains €16-22; ☽10am-midnight Mon-Thu, to 1.30am Fri & Sat; 🛜)

Restaurante Tenis Ondarreta
BASQUE €€

17 🍴 MAP P128, A3

At the foot of Monte Igueldo in the San Sebastián Royal Tennis Club,

Peine del Viento

A symbol of the city, the **Peine del Viento (Wind Comb) sculpture** (Map p128, A2; Paseo de Eduardo Chillida), which sits below Monte Igueldo at the far western end of the Bahía de la Concha, is the work of well-known Basque sculptor Eduardo Chillida and architect Luis Peña Ganchegui, and was installed in 1977. It makes for a great hour-long walk from the new town. On stormy days, waves crash between the rocks and add to the drama.

this restaurant has a white-dressed dining room and al fresco terrace overlooking the courts. Contemporary Basque dishes include garlicky salt-cod pil-pil with green-pepper sauce, grilled squid with parsley aioli, and cider-basted chicken with sweet potato. Start or end with a pint at the adjacent Wimbledon English pub. (943 31 11 50; www.tenisondarreta.com; Paseo de Eduardo Chillida 9; mains €18-20; 10am-5pm Tue & Wed, to 5pm & 8.30pm-midnight Thu-Sat, to 6pm Sun)

Casa Valles   PINTXOS €€

18 MAP P128, G4

Well away from the tourist hustle and bustle is this timber-panelled locals' institution with long communal tables, which serves some of the new town's best pintxos beneath a forest of hung hams.

Don't miss its gildas (anchovies, olives and pickled green peppers skewered on toothpicks), invented here in 1948. It also does raciones (sharing plates). (www.barvalles.com; Calle de los Reyes Católicos 10; pintxos €1.60-4.50; 1-3pm & 8.30-11pm)

Drinking

Bataplan Disco   CLUB

19 MAP P128, E4

San Sebastián's top club, a classic disco housed in a grand seafront complex, sets the stage for memorable beachside partying. The club action kicks in late, but in summer you can warm up with a drink or two on the street-level terrace. Note that door selection can be arbitrary and groups of men might have trouble getting in. (943 47 36 01; www.bataplandisco.com; Paseo de la Concha 12; club 12.30am-6am Thu, 11.30pm-6.30am Fri & Sat year-round, terrace 2pm-2.30am Jun-Sep)

Old Town Coffee   COFFEE

20 MAP P128, G4

The name is a misnomer but this new-town place is spot-on for coffee. Set up by two Brazilian friends, it does small-batch roasting on site, and uses boutique roasts such as Nomad (Barcelona) and Square Mile (London) in a variety of brewing techniques, including pour-overs, Aeropress and V20. Fresh-squeezed juices and all-day breakfasts (eg avocado toast) are also available (615 840753; Calle de los Reyes Católicos 6; 9am-6pm Tue-Sat, to 1pm Sun)

Gu COCKTAIL BAR

21 MAP P128, F2

Glorious beach views extend from this waterfront cocktail bar in the 1929-opened Real Club Náutico de San Sebastián building, designed to look like a boat. It's a stunning setting for a sundowner on the terrace and late-night cocktails. The DJ-fuelled club gets going at midnight. (843 980 775; www.gusansebastian.com; Calle Mari Ijentea 9; 5pm-2am Wed & Sun, to 5am Thu, to 6am Fri & Sat)

Pokhara BAR

22 MAP P128, H4

A hip favourite near the cathedral, Pokhara draws a wide cross section of imbibers and party people to its weekend DJ sessions. During the week, it's a fine spot to relax with a well-made cocktail, especially at the al fresco tables in front. Try the house-speciality *carajillo*, a hot espresso served with flaming whisky. (943 45 50 23; Calle de Sànchez Toca 1; 9am-2am Mon-Fri, from 3pm Sat & Sun)

Museo del Whisky BAR

23 MAP P128, G1

Appropriately named, this atmospheric bar is full of bottles of Scotland's finest (200 varieties are served) as well as a museum's worth of whisky-related knick-knacks displayed in timber-framed glass cabinets. (www.facebook.com/museodelwhisky; Alameda del Boulevard 5; 3.30pm-3.30am Mon-Sat)

Seafront, Playa de la Concha (p122)

SALVADOR AZNAR/SHUTTERSTOCK ©

San Sebastián New Town & Monte Igueldo Drinking

Pub Drop

CRAFT BEER

24 🚇 MAP P128, G4

One of a number of haunts on a popular drinking strip near the cathedral, Pub Drop is the place to get to grips with the local beer. There are up to 50 craft ales on offer, including 19 rotating on the taps. Try one of the brews from Basqueland Brewing Company, such as its Churros With Chocolate imperial stout. (📞943 35 98 57; Calle de los Reyes Católicos 18; 🕐4pm-midnight Mon-Thu, to 4am Fri, noon-4am Sat, to midnight Sun)

Botanika

CAFE

25 🚇 MAP P128, H3

Escape the beachfront hordes at this gem of a cafe. Housed in a river-facing residential block, it's popular with locals of all ages, who flock to the small, leafy patio and sunny, art-filled interior to chat over wine and vermouth. It also stages occasional live jazz, and DJs spin on summer Sundays. (www.facebook.com/kafe botanika; Paseo de Arból de Guernica 8; 🕐9am-11pm Mon-Thu, to midnight Fri & Sat, to 6pm Sun; 📶)

Koh Tao

CAFE

26 🚇 MAP P128, G2

Good at any time of the day, Koh Tao is a laid-back place with mismatched vintage furniture, comfy armchairs, street-art murals on its exposed-brick walls and good tunes. It's the ideal spot to unwind over a coffee or kick back with an early evening beer, wine or cocktail.

(📞943 42 22 11; Calle Bengoechea 2; 🕐7.30am-10pm Mon-Thu, to 2am Fri, 9am-2am Sat, to 10pm Sun; 📶)

La Mera Mera

BAR

27 🚇 MAP P128, A5

Just off the beaten path, La Mera Mera is a shoebox-sized bar with a bohemian air thanks to the old photos on the walls and slender brassy light fixtures. The cocktails are excellent (especially the pisco sours and strong margaritas), and the menu of Mexican snacks includes a smash-your-own guacamole. (www.lameramera.es; Calle de Matia 38; 🕐12.30pm-1am Sun-Tue & Thu, to 2am Fri & Sat)

Entertainment

Teatro Victoria Eugenia

THEATRE

28 ⭐ MAP P128, G1

Built in 1912 and refurbished between 2001 and 2007, the city's belle époque theatre presents a varied collection of theatre and classical music. A frescoed dome crowns its main hall, which has a capacity of 910 people. (📞943 48 11 60; www.victoriaeugenia.eus; Paseo de la República Argentina 2; 🕐box office 11.30am-1pm & 5-8pm)

Doka

LIVE MUSIC

29 ⭐ MAP P128, B5

Catch live music gigs in a wide range of genres – everything from Basque folk to rock, metal and pop – as well as theatre perfor-

Basque Cider

For the Basques, cider came before wine. The cool, rain-soaked hills of the Basque Country are ideal for growing apples, and where you find apples, you can bet you'll find cider as well. Basque cider is generally considered 'natural', in that it's not sparkling like most other European ciders. In order to add a little fizz, the cider is poured from wooden barrels into the glass from about arm's height.

A *sagardotegi* (*sidrería* in Spanish) is a cider house, one of the great institutions of Basque life. A *sagardotegi* isn't just about drinking cider, however, as they also serve food. Traditionally, a meal starts with a cod omelette, before moving onto charcoal-grilled steaks the size of a cow and finishing with dessert, which is invariably the local Idiazabal cheese with walnuts.

A night in a *sagardotegi* can be great fun. The average cost of a meal is around €25 to €30 per person, which includes all the cider you can drink. But you don't just go and get more cider as and when you please. Tradition states that each group of diners has someone who calls out '*txotx*' at regular intervals. This is your cue to get up from the table and head to the big barrels, where either a barman or the leader of your group opens the tap and everyone takes turns filling up before heading back to the table and awaiting the next round.

Cider season is January to April, but year-round it's possible to visit a number of orchards, manufacturers and cider houses. Find locations online at www.sagardoa.eus or ask at the **Sagardoetxea** (📞943 55 05 75; www.sagardoarenlurraldea.eus; Kale Nagusia 48, Astigarraga; adult/child €4/2; ⏰11am-1.30pm & 4-7.30pm Mon-Sat, 11am-1.30pm Sun Jul & Aug, closed Mon Sep-Jun), a cider museum, where you can tour an orchard, taste a tipple of cider and learn all you ever wanted to know about the drink. It's located on the edge of the little town of Astigarraga, 6km south of San Sebastián. Buses A1 and A2 run here from San Sebastián-Donostia Amara station (€1.80, 25 minutes, every 15 minutes).

mances, poetry readings and comedy. The small venue is in a residential backstreet just south of Playa de Ondarreta. (📞943 22 46 01; www.doka.eus; Calle Erregezain 20; ⏰9pm-2am Wed, 9pm-4.40am Thu, 8pm-6am Fri & Sat)

Shopping

Perfumería Benegas   PERFUME

30 🔒 MAP P128, G2

Founded in 1908, Benegas stocks leading international brands and in-house creations such

Riverside Walks

The Río Urumea runs through the middle of San Sebastián, separating the new town from the Gros neighbourhood. The river is largely overlooked by visitors, but locals love to stroll the walkways that run along the banks, scattered with small areas of parkland and children's playgrounds.

as Ssirimiri, which uses San Sebastián as its inspiration – the rains, sunshine and sea breezes all packaged in one lovely box. You'll also find make-up and gents' grooming products. (www.perfumeriabenegas.com; Calle de Garibai 12; ⏰10am-1.15pm & 4-8pm Mon-Sat)

Mimo San Sebastián Gourmet Shop
FOOD & DRINKS

Located inside the regal Hotel Maria Cristina, this is where those with a real appreciation of fine food and wine come to do their shopping. The shop (see 4 🔘 Map p128, H2) also offers customised hampers and international shipping, as well as a wide selection of edible souvenirs, tableware and gourmet gifts. Check out Mimo's foodie tours (p25) and cooking classes as well. (www.mimofood.com; Paseo de la República Argentina 4, Hotel Maria Cristina; ⏰10am-8pm Mon-Fri, to 7pm Sat & Sun)

Loreak Mendian
CLOTHING

31 🔒 MAP P128, G2

Basque label Loreak Mendian specialises in affordable style for men and women – everything from T-shirts and hoodies to dresses and lightweight sweaters. This branch carries menswear, while its shop around the corner at Calle de Garibai 22 has women's fashions. (www.loreakmendian.com; Calle de Hernani 27; ⏰10.30am-8pm Mon-Sat)

Erviti
MUSICAL INSTRUMENTS

32 🔒 MAP P128, G3

Erviti has published Basque musical scores since it was established in 1875. Now run by the fifth generation, it stocks traditional Basque musical instruments, including an *alboka* (single-reed woodwind instrument), *txistu* (three-holed wooden pipe), *ttun-ttun* (six-stringed instrument named for the sound it makes) and a *kirikoketa* and *txalaparta* (both wooden percussion instruments similar to xylophones). (www.erviti.com; Calle de San Martín 28; ⏰10am-1.30pm & 4-8pm Mon-Fri, 10am-1.30pm Sat)

Chocolates de Mendaro
CHOCOLATE

33 🔒 MAP P128, H2

It's all but impossible to walk past this fabulous old chocolate shop and resist the temptation to step inside. The famed chocolatier has been around since 1850 and is still run by the Saint-Gerons family. (www.chocolatesdemendaro.com; Calle de Etxaide 6; 🕙10am-1.30pm & 4.30-8pm Mon-Fri, 10am-1.30pm Sat)

Elkano 1 Gaztagune   CHEESE

34 🔒 MAP P128, G2

Over 40 different artisan cheeses fill this aromatic little timber-lined shop. Most are from the Basque Country, including the owner's own Idiazabal (pressed sheep's milk cheese); there are also a handful of varieties from France, Italy, the Netherlands and Scotland. (www.facebook.com/elkano1 gaztagune; Calle Elkano 1; 🕙10am-2pm & 4-8.15pm Mon-Sat)

Mercado San Martín   MARKET

35 🔒 MAP P128, G3

Originally built in 1884, Mercado San Martín was replaced with a gleaming modern structure in 2005. At street level you'll find butchers, greengrocers, florists and a excellent bakery, as well as cafes. Downstairs is a large fishmonger's hall filled with locally caught seafood. (www.mercadosanmartin.es; Calle de Urbieta 9; 🕙8am-8pm Mon-Sat)

Goiuri   FASHION & ACCESSORIES

36 🔒 MAP P128, G4

If you're looking for a new statement-making swimsuit to wear on the beach, head to Goiuri. It stocks its own bikinis and one-pieces for women and Sargori board shorts for men, which it designs and produces locally, as well as women's swimwear from Australian brand Seafolly. (www.goiuri.com; Calle San Bartolomé 9; 🕙10am-1pm & 4-8pm Mon-Sat)

Puente de Santa Catalina

San Sebastián Gros

The seaside neighbourhood of Gros is cool, young and pure surf fashion. The neighbourhood largely lacks the architectural pleasures of other parts of town, but with a spectacular beach, some of the best-value hotels in the city and a reputation as a pintxo powerhouse, you're likely to spend a lot of time having fun here.

The Short List

o **Playa de la Zurriola (p143)** Strolling Gros' sweeping surf beach at sunset.

o **Parque de Cristina Enea (p143)** Escaping the crowds in the city's prettiest park, among peacocks, towering trees and expanses of lawn.

o **Kursaal (p146)** Checking out the futuristic design – two cubes made of translucent glass with LED lights – of architect Rafael Moneo's striking cultural centre.

o **Pintxos (p144)** Dining on bite-size delights along restaurant-lined Calle de Peña y Goñi.

o **Water sports (p143)** Hiring a board – or taking a class – to ride the waves lapping at Gros' doorstep.

Getting There & Around

🏃 Gros is just over the Puente de Zurriola (Zurriola Bridge), which leads to the Parte Vieja and the new town. There's no need to use public transport to get here.

Neighbourhood Map on p142

Pintxos, San Sebastián RRRAINBOW/SHUTTERSTOCK ©

San Sebastián Gros

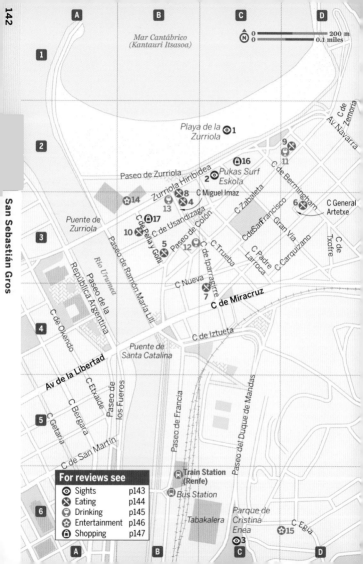

Mar Cantábrico
(Kantauri Itsasoa)

N 0 ———— 200 m
   0 ———— 0.1 miles

Playa de la **1**
Zurriola

16
Pukas Surf **2**
Eskola
Paseo de Zurriola
Zurriola Hiribidea
14 **8** C Miguel Imaz
13 **4**
17
10 **5**
C de Peña y Goñi
C de Usandizaga
Paseo de Colón
12

9
11
C de Bermingham
C Zabaleta
CdeSanFrancisco
Gran Vía
C Padre
Larroca
C de Carquizano

6
C General
Artetxe
C de
Txofre

Puente de
Zurriola

Río Urumea

Paseo de la
República Argentina

Paseo de Ramón María Lili

C de Iparragirre
C de Trueba
C Nueva
7
C de Miracruz

C de Iztueta

Puente de
Santa Catalina

C de Okendo

Av de la Libertad

C de Etxaide
Paseo de
los Fueros
C Bergara
C Getaria
C de San Martín

Paseo de Francia

Paseo del Duque de Mandas

Train Station
(Renfe)
Bus Station

Tabakalera

Parque de
Cristina
Enea

15

C Egia

3

Sights

Playa de la Zurriola BEACH

1  MAP P142, C2

Stretching 800m in front of Gros, from the Kursaal to Monte Ulía, 'Zurri', as it's known locally, has some excellent waves that draw surfers from near and far. It's a superb place to hang out and take in the local scene of volleyball, football and surf action; swimming here is at its best when there's no swell.

Pukas Surf Eskola SURFING

2  MAP P142, C2

Aspiring surfers should drop by Pukas. Prices for classes vary depending on duration and

group size, but start at €68 for a weekend course comprising a 1½-hour lesson each day. It also hires boards and wetsuits. (☎943 32 00 68; www.pukassurf.com; Zurriola Hiribidea 24; ☺9am-2pm & 4-8pm Mon-Sat, 9am-2.30pm Sun)

Parque de Cristina Enea PARK

3  MAP P142, C6

Created by the Duke of Mandas in honour of his wife, the Parque de Cristina Enea is a favourite escape for locals. This formal park, the most attractive in the city, contains ornamental plants, ducks and peacocks, and open lawns. Its wooded paths make for a lovely scenic stroll, past towering red sequoias and a magnificent

Playa de la Zurriola and the gleaming Kursaal (p146)

Lebanese cedar. (Paseo Duque de Mandas; ⏱8am-9pm May-Sep, 9am-7pm Oct-Apr)

Eating

Xarma

BASQUE €€

4 ✖ MAP P142, B3

A striking contemporary wood-lined dining room with bare-bulb downlighting is the backdrop for artistically presented dishes prepared in the open kitchen. A meal might start with watermelon gazpacho with melon-filled cucumber cannelloni, followed by smoked Basque trout with Ossau-Iraty sheep's cheese, fresh herbs and honey, or suckling pig's trotters with roast onion cream and caramelised figs. (☎943 14 22 67; www.xarmacook.com; Calle Miguel Imaz 1; mains €16-26; ⏱1-3.30pm Tue & Sun, 1-3.30pm & 8.30-11.15pm Wed-Sat)

Bodega Donostiarra

PINTXOS €

5 ✖ MAP P142, B3

The whitewashed stone walls, framed prints and black-and-white photos give this place a quirky charm, though the crowds can be so thick that you might not even notice during prime time. The draw? Some of the best *pintxos* this side of the Urumea: seared mackerel with salmon roe, black pudding with sweet red peppers, or grilled chorizo and octopus skewers. (☎943 01 13 80; www.bodega donostiarra.com; Calle de Peña y Goñi 13; pintxos €2-4; ⏱9.30am-4pm & 7-11pm Mon-Thu, to midnight Fri & Sat)

Bergara Bar

PINTXOS €

6 ✖ MAP P142, D3

The Bergara Bar is one of Gros' most highly regarded *pintxo* bars and has a mouth-watering array of delights piled on the bar counter, as well as others chalked on the board. You can't go wrong, whether you opt for its anchovy tortilla, *chupito* (spider crab mousse served in a shot glass) or rich foie gras with mango jam. (www.pinchos bergara.es; General Artetxe 8; pintxos €2-4.50; ⏱9.30am-11pm)

Gerald's Bar

INTERNATIONAL €€

7 ✖ MAP P142, C4

Melbourne-based restaurateur Gerald Diffey fell so hard for San Sebastián that he decided to open a second Gerald's in the city – never mind that the first is 17,000km away. The menu changes daily but might feature steak-and-kidney pie, smoked duck breast with fig and red-onion chutney, or roast butternut squash with labneh (yogurt) and pistachio pesto. (☎943 08 30 01; www.geralds bar.eu; Calle de Iparragirre 13; mains €12-20; ⏱1-4pm & 7-11pm Tue-Sun)

Loaf

BAKERY €

8 ✖ MAP P142, B3

Streetside viewing windows let you watch the Loaf baking breads, cakes (eg lemon drizzle), cookies and other treats, including rich, dense chocolate brownies. Beginning life as a shipping container pop-up, it now has a handful of branches around San Sebastián. This flagship Gros branch also incorporate a sit-down cafe serving salads, *tostas* (open-faced toasties) and sandwiches. (www.theloaf.eus; Zurriola Hiribidea 18; pastries €1-5.50; dishes €3.50-6.50; ⏰9am-8pm; 🛜)

La Guinda

CAFE €€

9 ✕ MAP P142, D2

The pick of the seats at this little cafe a block from the beach are on the terrace, shaded by a retractable awning. Breakfast dishes range from yogurt with seasonal fruit to bacon and eggs. Daily lunch specials traverse the globe: wok-fried noodle dishes, codfish tacos, pulled pork with mango, avocado and cilantro, and vegetarian lasagne with broccoli and spinach. (📞843 98 17 15; www.laguindadelicoffee.com; Calle Zabaleta 55; mains €10-22; ⏰8am-6pm Tue-Fri, 9am-6pm Sat, to 5pm Sun; 🖊)

Le Comidare

INTERNATIONAL €

10 ✕ MAP P142, B3

On one of Gros' liveliest eating strips, Le Comidare has a minimalist, Scandinavian aesthetic with light wood tables, downlighting, a long wall of artwork and concrete floors. It draws a crowd at all hours for burritos, bagels, burgers, sandwiches and sharing plates. You'll also find craft brews and good wine selections. (📞943 84 77 32; Calle de Peña y Goñi 4; mains €8-13; ⏰noon-midnight Sun-Thu, to 1am Fri & Sat)

San Sebastián to Pasaia on Foot

A rewarding way of reaching Pasaia (p153) is to walk the coastal path from San Sebastián. This 7.7km trail, part of the Camino del Norte, takes about three hours and passes patches of forest and unusual cliff formations, offering lovely sea views. Halfway along, a hidden beach, Playa de Murgita, tempts when it's hot.

From San Sebastián, the route starts at the eastern end of Gros' Playa de la Zurriola, at the top of the steps leading from Calle de Zemoria up Monte Ulía. From Pasaia it climbs past the lighthouse on the western side of the port.

Drinking

Mala Gissona Beer House

CRAFT BEER

11 🍺 MAP P142, D2

The long wooden bar, industrial fixtures and inviting front terrace make a suitable backdrop to the dozen quality brews on tap. Half are from its own brewery in nearby Oiartzun, such as Nao (pale ale) and Django (blanche), while the others are from other Basque and international brewers. Soak them up with bar food including fantastic burgers. (www.malagissona.beer; Calle Zabaleta 53; ⏰5-11.30pm Mon,

San Sebastián's Cultural Centre

Sun-drenched cultural space **Tabakalera** (International Centre for Contemporary Culture; Map p142, C6; 📞 943 11 88 55; www. tabakalera.eu; Plaza Andre Zigarrogileak 1; ⏱ 9am-9pm Mon-Thu, to 10pm Fri & Sun, 10am-10pm Sat Sep-Jun, to 11pm Fri & Sat Jul & Aug) occupies a beautifully reconfigured tobacco factory. It's a hub for the arts and design, as well as cultural enterprises such as the Basque Film Archive, the Kutxa Foundation and various galleries and innovative firms. For visitors, there's also an exhibition hall, a cinema and a regular line-up of seminars, workshops, discussions and other edifying fare. There's always something going on; check online or stop by for the latest.

1-11.30pm Tue-Thu, to 1.30am Fri & Sat, noon-12.30am Sun; 📶)

La Gintonería Donostiarra

BAR

12 🚇 MAP P142, B3

A much-loved drinking spot in Gros, this gin joint has more than 100 varieties of the good stuff, and makes one of the best (and biggest!) gin and tonics in town. The all-white interior is light, bright and contemporary; on warm days, the best seats are out on the terrace. (www. facebook.com/lagintoneriadonostiarra;

Calle Zabaleta 6; ⏱ 3pm-2am Tue-Thu & Sun, to 3.30am Fri & Sat; 📶)

Bar Ondarra

BAR

13 🚇 MAP P142, B3

Across the road from Playa de la Zurriola, Bar Ondarra draws a chilled-out surf crowd. Live music gigs often take place in the basement. (Zurriola Hiribidea 16; ⏱ 11am-1am Tue-Sun)

Entertainment

Kursaal

LIVE PERFORMANCE

14 ⭐ MAP P142, B3

An energetic and exciting array of performances are staged inside the Kursaal centre, an architectural landmark dating to 1999. Everything from symphonic concerts and musicals to dance performances and rock shows features; check out the website for upcoming events. (📞 943 00 30 00; www.kursaal.eus; Zurriola Hiribidea 1)

Le Bukowski

LIVE MUSIC

15 ⭐ MAP P142, D6

Live bands take the stage most nights at this nightspot, which also has DJs spinning a wide range of sounds – funk, hip-hop, soul, rock. It's located south of Gros near the mainline train station. (www.lebukowski.com; Calle Egia 18; ⏱ 10am-11pm Mon-Wed, to 2am Thu, to 4am Fri, 7pm-4am Sat, 7pm-midnight Sun; 📶)

Shopping

Shopping

Kañabikaña ALCOHOL

16 🔒 MAP P142, C2

You can buy Basque and guest international craft beers to take away at Kañabikaña, or fill a take-away bottle (330ml, 500ml or 1000ml) from one of its 18 taps and head to the beach (it's not licensed for drinking on site). (www.kainabikaina.com; Zurriola Hiribidea 36; ⏱5-10pm Mon, noon-2.30pm & 5-10pm Tue-Sun)

Hitz FASHION & ACCESSORIES

17 🔒 MAP P142, B3

On one of Gros' liveliest lanes, this women's wear boutique is a great place to hit up when you need a new piece for your travel wardrobe. Browse for soft linen shirts, over-sized sweaters, leather jackets, printed scarves and rugged canvas bags with leather straps. (www.hitz.es; Calle de Peña y Goñi 1; ⏱10am-2pm & 4-8pm Mon-Fri, 10am-2pm Sat)

La Gintonería Donostiarra

Explore ◉
Hondarribia & Pasaia

With its walled Casco Histórico (Historic Centre), buzzing beach scene and fabulous eateries, Hondarribia makes for a wonderful day trip or longer visit. The town, 20km from San Sebastián on the French border, lies to the east of the historic port of Pasaia.

The Short List

○ **Casco Histórico (p151)** *Wandering through Hondarribia's historic core.*

○ **Ermita de Guadalupe (p152)** *Hiking up to this hilltop hermitage to take in magnificent views.*

○ **Hendaye (p154)** *Hopping aboard the ferry from Hondarribia to this beautiful sandy beach across the border in France.*

○ **Albaola Foundation (p153)** *Learning about Pasaia's whaling history at this fascinating maritime museum.*

○ **Casa Museo Victor Hugo (p153)** *Visiting the former Pasaia base of writer Victor Hugo.*

Getting There & Around

🚌 Buses link Hondarribia's Calle Sabin Arana with the bus station in San Sebastián (€2.65, 25 minutes, every 30 minutes).

🚢 To cross over to France, take the Hendaye–Hondarribia passenger ferry.

Neighbourhood Map on p150

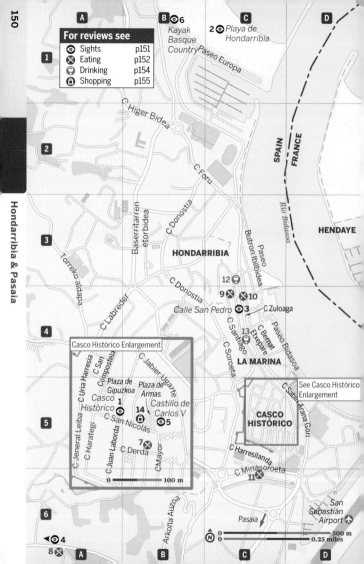

For reviews see

⊙	Sights	p151
⊗	Eating	p152
⊜	Drinking	p154
🔒	Shopping	p155

B ⊙6
Kayak
Basque
Country

2 ⊙ Playa de
Hondarribia

Paseo Europa

C. Higer Bidea

SPAIN
FRANCE

Río Bidasoa

HENDAYE

C. Foru

Baserritarren
etorbidea

C. Donostia

HONDARRIBIA

Torreko aldapa

C. Labreder

C. Donostia

12 ⊜

9 ⊗   ⊗10

Calle San Pedro ⊙3   C Zuloaga

Buttron Ibilbidea

Paseo
Bidasoa

13
Bernat
Etxepare

C Bernat

C Santiago

C Soroeta

LA MARINA

Casco Histórico Enlargement

C Jabier Ugarte

C San
Compostela

C. Uria Harresia

Plaza de
Gipuzkoa

Plaza de
Armas

Casco
Histórico

1 ⊙

14
🔒

Castillo de
Carlos V

⊙5

See Casco Histórico
Enlargement

C Sabin Arana Gori

CASCO
HISTÓRICO

C Jeneral Leiba

C Haretgi

C Juan Laborda

C San Nicólas

7 ⊗

C Derda

C Mayor

C Harresilanda

C Minasoroeta

11 ⊗

0 ——— 100 m

Arkolla Auzoa

Pasaia

San
Sebastián
Airport

N
0 ——— 500 m
0 ——— 0.25 miles

⊙4

8 ⊗

A   B   C   D

Sights

Casco Histórico OLD TOWN

1 ⊙ MAP P150, A5

Hondarribia's walled historic centre, much of which dates to the 15th and 16th centuries, is an atmospheric grid of graceful plazas, cobbled lanes, and buildings adorned with wood-carved eaves and wrought-iron balconies. The focal square is **Plaza de Armas**, where you'll find the local **tourist office** (📞630 462948; www.hondarribiaturismo.com; Plaza de Armas 9; ⊙9.30am-7.30pm Jul–mid-Sep, 10am-6pm Mon-Sat & 10am-2pm Sun mid-Sep–Jun), but prettier still is picture-perfect **Plaza de Gipuzkoa**.

Playa de Hondarribia BEACH

2 ⊙ MAP P150, C1

Hondarribia's sheltered beach is lined with bars and restaurants, and offers calm swimming waters. When the swell is running, there's a long right-hand surf break off the breakwater. Located 2km north of the new town (La Marina), the beach is popular with locals, but foreign tourists are rare.

Calle San Pedro STREET

3 ⊙ MAP P150, C4

The main drag of Hondarribia's La Marina district, Calle San Pedro is a quaint pedestrian-only strip flanked by traditional fishers' houses, with facades painted bright green or blue, and wooden balconies cheerfully decorated

Beachside promenade, Hondarribia

with flower boxes. Many of the old-fashioned buildings now contain *pintxo* bars and restaurants.

Ermita de Guadalupe   CHAPEL

4 ⊙ MAP P150, A6

It's a hefty hike from Hondarribia – a 4km walk uphill – but the Ermita de Guadalupe is well worth the effort it takes to reach it (you can also drive) and has stunning views. Destroyed and rebuilt many times over the centuries, the hermitage's present structure dates from the 19th century. Pick up a walking trail map from the tourist office. A pilgrimage takes place here on 8 September. (Guadalupe Hermitage; Carretera Jaizkibel, GI-3440; ⊙9am-1pm & 4-7pm)

Castillo de Carlos V   CASTLE

5 ⊙ MAP P150, B5

Today it's a government-run hotel, but for over 1000 years this castle hosted knights and kings. Its position atop the old town hill gave it a commanding view over the strategic Bidasoa estuary, which has long marked the Spain–France border. Poke your head into the reception lobby to admire the medieval decor. (Plaza de Armas 14)

Kayak Basque Country   KAYAKING

6 ⊙ MAP P150, B1

Kayaking trips run by this long-established operator include a one-hour sunset estuary tour, a two-hour trip around Isla de Amuitz with the option of snorkelling, and

a three-hour descent along the Bidasoa river. It also arranges three-hour fishing trips. (☑679 600839; www.kayakbasquecountry.com; Paseo Europa, Playa de Hondarribia; tours €18-48; ⊙by appointment)

Eating

Gastroteka Danontzat   BASQUE €€

7 ✖ MAP P150, B5

Gastroteka Danontzat's fun, creative approach to dining combines beautifully prepared market-fresh fare with highly original presentation and props. Start off with smoked sardines, anchovies or crab croquettes, before moving on to tender tuna ceviche, squid cooked in its own ink or chargrilled entrecôte in red-pepper sauce. Small servings mean you can try a lot of flavours. (☑943 64 65 97; www.gastrotekadanontzat.com; Calle Denda 6; small plates €8-18; ⊙noon-4pm & 7.30pm-midnight Mon & Thu-Sun, 7.30pm-midnight Wed)

Laía Erretegia   GRILL €€€

8 ✖ MAP P150, A6

Chef Jon Ayala and his maître d' sister Arantxa transformed these former stables into an open-plan dining space with glass cabinets where beef is aged for 30 to 60 days, wraparound shelves stocked with wine, and floor-to-ceiling windows overlooking the surrounding farmland and mountains. Steaks and daily caught seafood are grilled over charcoal; vegetables come

Visiting
Pasaia

Where the river Oiartzun meets the Atlantic, Pasaia (Spanish: Pasajes) is both a massive industrial port and a sleepy village with quaint medieval houses hunkering over the waterfront. In fact, it comprises four distinct districts, though it's Pasai San Pedro and Pasai Donibane that have all the charm. These two villages face each other on opposite sides of the river, linked by a frequent, three-minute **ferry** (Map p150; one-way €0.80; ⏰6.30am-11pm Mon-Thu, to midnight Fri, 7am-midnight Sat, 7.45am-11pm Sun) ride, and are sprinkled with sights that pay homage to the region's maritime history.

The **Albaola Foundation** (Map p142; ☎943 39 24 26; www.albaola. com; Ondartxo Ibilbida 1, Pasai San Pedro; adult/child €7/5; ⏰10am-2pm & 3-7pm Tue-Sun Easter–mid-Sep, to 6pm mid-Sep–Easter) charts the history of Pasaia's whaling industry. At the centre of the story is the *San Juan*, a galleon that sunk off the coast of Newfoundland in 1565. Models and explanatory panels describe the ship and illustrate how a team of Canadian underwater archaeologists discovered its wreck in 1978. The highlight, though, is the life-size replica of the ship that they are building using the same techniques and materials that were used to construct the original.

French author Victor Hugo spent the summer of 1843 in Pasaia, lodging at the 17th-century waterfront house that's now the **Casa Museo Victor Hugo** (☎943 34 15 56; Calle Donibane 63, Pasai Donibane; admission free; ⏰9am-2pm & 4-7pm Jul & Aug, 10am-2pm & 4-6pm Tue-Sat, to 2pm Sun Sep-Jun). The 2nd floor retains a smattering of period furniture and various prints and first editions. The 1st floor is home to Pasaia's **tourist office** (Map p150; ☎943 34 15 56; www.oarsoaldea turismoa.eus; Calle Donibane 63, Pasai Donibane; ⏰9am-2pm & 4-7pm Jul & Aug, 10am-2pm & 4-6pm Tue-Sat, to 2pm Sun Sep-Jun).

Seafood is the star of the area's menus. Managed by the same family since 1884, **Casa Cámara** (☎943 52 36 99; www.casacamara.com; Calle San Juan 79, Pasai Donibane; mains €19-33; ⏰1.30-3.30pm Tue, Wed & Sun, 1.30-3.30pm & 8.30-10.30pm Thu-Sat) is built half on stilts over the harbour. The majority of the menu is seafood based and the cooking is assured and traditional. The lobsters live in a cage lowered down through a hole in the middle of the dining area straight into the water.

Buses link Hondarribia with Pasai San Pedro (€2.65, 30 minutes, every 30 minutes). You can also reach Pasai San Pedro directly from San Sebastián's bus station (€1.80, 10 minutes, every 30 minutes) or on foot (p145) from Gros.

Gallic Hendaye

Just across the river from Hondarribia lies the pretty French town of Hendaye, linked by a regular passenger **ferry** (www.jolaski.com; Paseo Button Ibilbidea; one-way €2; ⏱ every 15 min 10am-1am Jul–mid-Sep, 10.15am-7pm Mon-Fri, to 8pm Sat & Sun Apr-Jun & mid-Sep–late Sep, shorter hours Oct-Mar). Apart from nibbling on perfectly flaky croissants, Hendaye's main attraction is its 3km-long stretch of white-sand beach, a 250m stroll north of the ferry dock. It's protected by a headland that ensures calm waters for swimming.

from within a 30km radius. (☎943 64 63 09; www.laiaerretegia.com; Arkolla Auzoa 33; mains €22-40; ⏱1-3pm Mon-Thu, 1-3pm & 8.30-10pm Fri, 1.30-3pm & 8.30-10pm Sat, 1.30-3pm Sun)

Gran Sol   PINTXOS €

9 ❌ MAP P150, C4

Wine barrels double as tables out the front of Gran Sol, one of Hondarribia's best-known spots for *pintxos*. Standouts include mushrooms filled with cheese mousse, smoked cod with foie gras and peach jam, and pork three ways. Along with *txakoli* and other local wines, it has a range of Basque craft beers. (☎943 64 27 01; www.bargransol.com; Calle San Pedro 65; pintxos €2-4.80; ⏱12.30-3.30pm & 8.30-10.30pm Tue-Sun)

La Hermandad de Pescadores   SEAFOOD €€€

10 ❌ MAP P150, C4

Housed in a traditional white-and-blue cottage, this institution dating to 1938 serves an array of seafood classics. It's best known for its *sopa de pescado* (fish soup), said by some to be the best in the area. (☎943 64 27 38; www.hermandad depescadores.com; Calle Zuloaga 12; mains €18-45; ⏱1-3.30pm & 8-10.30pm Tue-Sat, 1-3.30pm Sun)

Alameda   BASQUE €€€

11 ❌ MAP P150, C6

Michelin-starred Alameda helped pave the way to Hondarribia becoming the culinary hotspot it is today. What started life as a simple tavern is now a sophisticated fine-dining restaurant, complete with a garden and terrace, serving creative takes on traditional Basque cuisine. (☎943 64 27 89; www.restaurantealameda.net; Calle Minasoroeta 1; tasting menus €78-115; ⏱noon-3.30pm Tue-Thu & Sun, noon-3.30pm & 7.30-11pm Fri & Sat)

Drinking

Vinoteka Ardoka   WINE BAR

12 🍷 MAP P150, C3

Behind its rustic stone facade, this contemporary wine bar has 50 wines by the glass, including *txakoli*, Tempranillo from Navarra, and reds and rosés from La Rioja, as well as over a dozen varieties of vermouth. Pair them with *pintxos* such as *txipiron* (squid-ink croquettes), *bacalao confitado* (confit cod) and *alcachofas fritas* (fried artichokes). (www.ardokavinoteka.com; Calle San Pedro 32; ⏱11.30am-3.30pm & 6-11.30pm Jul & Aug, closed Tue Sep-Jun)

Amona Margarita   CAFE

13 🚇 MAP P150, C4

With a light, airy interior, this cafe-bakery is a lovely place to rejuvenate with a freshly squeezed juice, coffee or home-baked cake. (www.amonamargarita.com; Calle San Pedro 4; ⏱7.30am-9pm Mon-Fri, 8am-9pm Sat & Sun; 📶)

Shopping

Conservas Hondarribia   FOOD & DRINKS

14 🔒 MAP P150, B5

Everything at this light, bright deli is sourced within 150km of Hondarribia: salted anchovies, tinned sardines, clams and octopus, cheeses, preserved chillies, vinegar, oils, honey, chocolate, craft beers, liqueurs, wines and more. (www.conservashondarribia.com; Plaza de Armas 8; ⏱11am-7pm Thu-Mon)

Hondarribia's Casco Histórico (p151)

TOKAR/SHUTTERSTOCK ©

Walking Tour

St-Jean de Luz, France

A short hop across the French border, St-Jean de Luz is a picturesque seaside village with a lively waterfront, impressive historic sights, and narrow cobblestone lanes that invite exploring. While this 1km walk takes around an hour, you could easily make a day of it, hanging out at the beach, followed by dining and drinking at the town's superb seafood restaurants.

Getting There

🚌 Ouibus (www.ouibus.com) connects St-Jean de Luz with San Sebastián's bus station (€5-15 one way, 40 minutes, six daily).

🚗 Take the AP8, which becomes the A63 as you cross into France.

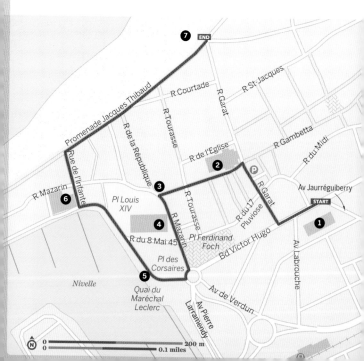

❶ Les Halles Centrales

Dating from 1884, the town's grand **market** (bd Victor Hugo; ⏰7am-1pm) offers a delight for the senses, with its vendors selling fresh fruits, cheeses, cured meats, breads and pastries. A corner food stall serves grilled sardines, oysters and refreshing wine.

❷ Église St-Jean Baptiste

The plain facade of France's largest Basque **church** (www.paroissespo.com/eglise-st-jean-baptiste-st-jean-de-luz/; rue Gambetta; ⏰8.30am-6pm Mon-Sat, 8am-7.30pm Sun) conceals a splendid interior with a magnificent baroque altarpiece. Louis XIV and María Teresa, daughter of King Philip IV of Spain, married here in 1660.

❸ Maison Adam

At the entrance to lively shopping and dining strip rue de la République, **Maison Adam** (☏05 59 26 03 54; www.maisonadam.fr; 6 rue de la République; ⏰8am-12.30pm & 2-7.30pm) has been selling delicious *gâteau basque* (Basque cake filled with almond cream or preserved cherries) since 1666. It also has macarons, wines and preserves.

❹ Maison Louis XIV

The grandest house in town is the **Maison Louis XIV** (☏05 59 26 27 58; www.maison-louis-xiv.fr; 6 place Louis XIV; adult/child €6.50/4; ⏰10.30am-12.30pm & 2.30-6.30pm Wed-Mon Jul & Aug, 11.30am-3pm & 4-5pm Wed-Mon Easter, Jun & Sep–

mid-Oct), where Louis XIV lived out his last days of bachelorhood. It was built in 1643 by a wealthy ship-owner, and is awash with period detail and antiques. Guided tours depart regularly.

❺ Fishing Port

Centuries of history lie hidden in this colourful fishing port. From here ships headed off to hunt whales off the frigid coast of Newfoundland in the 16th century. Although Saint-Jean de Luz has been a resort since the 19th century, it still has an active fishing fleet – though these days it goes after smaller catch.

❻ Maison de l'Infante

In the days before her marriage to Louis XIV, María Teresa stayed in this brick-and-stone **mansion** (☏05 59 26 36 82; 1 rue de l'Infante; adult/child €2.50/2; ⏰2.30-6.30pm Mon, 11am-12.30pm & 2.30-6.30pm Tue-Sat Jun–mid-Nov), just off place Louis XIV. Like her husband-to-be's temporary home, it was constructed by a shipowner.

❼ Grande Plage

The lovely crescent-shaped sands of the Grande Plage make a fine setting for a bit of downtime. Protected from the battering waves of the Atlantic by three breakwaters, the beach has calm waters, perfect for young swimmers. A long elevated promenade offers beautiful views over the seaside.

Survival Guide

Puente de Maria Cristina (p131), San Sebastián

Before You Go

Book Your Stay

o Hotel rooms are at a premium in Basque Country, particularly in San Sebastián.

o Availability in high season is tight. During Easter and from June to September, book months in advance.

Useful Websites

o **Lonely Planet** (lonely planet.com/spain/hotels) Recommendations and bookings.

o **Tourism Euskadi** (www.tourism.euskadi.eus) The Basque tourist board gives lots of accommodation suggestions.

o **Bilbao Turismo** (www.bilbaoturismo.net) Accommodation bookings from Bilbao's tourism authority.

o **San Sebastián Turismo** (www.sansebastian turismo.com) Bookings from San Sebastián's tourism authority.

o **Feel Free Rentals** (www.feelfreerentals.

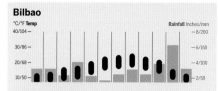

When to Go

o **Spring (Mar–May)** Unpredictable, sometimes very wet weather. May is more reliably sunny. Tourist crowds are low.

o **Summer (Jun–Sep)** Hot, endless festivals. Waves of tourists, higher prices.

o **Autumn (Oct & Nov)** October can be glorious, but by November winter is coming.

o **Winter (Dec–Feb)** Wet, often cold. Some sights are closed or operate on reduced hours.

com) San Sebastián–based outfit renting apartments in and near the city.

Best Budget

Poshtel Bilbao (www.poshtelbilbao.com) Flashpacker base with first-rate facilities including a restaurant, bar and sauna.

Quartier Bilbao (www.quartierbilbao.com) A good-value penny pincher in Bilbao's old quarter.

Koba (www.kobahostel.com) Surfer-friendly hostel in San

Sebastián's Gros neighbourhood.

Itsasmin Ostatua (www.itsasmin.com) In the hillside village of Elantxobe.

Pensión Txiki Polit (www.txikipolit.eus) Old-fashioned charm close to the beach in Zarautz' old town.

Best Midrange

Pensión Altair (www.pension-altair.com) Converted San Sebastián townhouse near the eateries of Gros.

Pensión Aldamar (www.pensionaldamar.

com) Professionally run, contemporary guesthouse in an excellent San Sebastián location.

Pensión Iturrienea Ostatua (www.iturrieneaostatua.com) Whimsically decorated *pensión* in Bilbao's old town; full of good cheer.

Casual Bilbao Gurea (www.casualhoteles.com) Family-run guesthouse near some great eating options in Bilbao's old town.

Hotel Ilunion Bilbao (www.ilunionbilbao.com) Well-priced contemporary hotel with all the essentials for a relaxing stay.

Hotel Zubieta (www.hotelzubieta.com) Lovely boutique hotel in the seaside village of Lekeitio.

Best Top End

Hotel Carlton (www.hotelcarlton.es) Grande dame of Bilbao with classic rooms and top-notch service.

Hotel Maria Cristina (www.hotel-maria cristina.com) The most famous address in San Sebastián, with stellar service and lavish rooms.

Miró Hotel (www.mirohotelbilbao.com) Stylish boutique accommodation across from the Museo Guggenheim Bilbao.

Gran Hotel Domine (www.granhoteldominebilbao.com) Luxury Bilbao hotel with all the frills, including a scenic roof terrace.

Hotel de Londres y de Inglaterra (www.hlondres.com) A majestic hotel with mesmerising views over San Sebastián's Playa de la Concha.

Hotel Iturregi (www.hoteliturregi.com) Ultracontemporary opulence in the hills above Getaria with sweeping Basque Coast views.

Arriving in Bilbao & San Sebastián

Bilbao Airport

○ Bilbao Airport (www.aena.es) is 13km northeast of the centre.

○ The **airport bus** (Biz-

kaibus A3247; one-way €3) departs from a stand on the extreme right as you leave arrivals.

○ It travels through the northwestern section of the city, passing the Museo Guggenheim Bilbao, stopping at Plaza de Federico Moyúa and terminating at the Intermodal bus station.

○ Services run from the airport every 15 minutes to 30 minutes from 6.15am to midnight.

○ There is also a direct hourly bus from the airport to San Sebastián's bus station, adjacent to the mainline train station (€17.10, 1¼ hours). It runs every 30 minutes from 7.15am to 11.45pm.

○ Taxis from the airport to the Casco Viejo cost about €25 to €35 depending on traffic.

San Sebastián Airport

○ San Sebastián Airport (www.aena.es) is 22km east of town, near Hondarribia.

○ It is a domestic airport serving Madrid and Barcelona.

○ Buses E20 and E21 run hourly to San Sebastián's bus station

(€2.65, 30 minutes), stopping at Plaza de Gipuzkoa.

○ A taxi from the airport to the city centre costs about €35 to €45.

Biarritz Airport

○ Biarritz Airport (www. biarritz.aeroport.fr), 48km northeast of San Sebastián in France, is a convenient arrival point for the region.

○ Destinations served include the UK, Ireland and major continental European cities.

○ Buses (€7, 45 minutes, up to eight daily) link

the airport with San Sebastián's bus station.

From the Train Stations

○ Bilbao's Abando train station is just across the river from Plaza Arriaga and the Casco Viejo.

○ Most accommodation is an easy walk away, but if you're staying near the Museo Guggenheim Bilbao, you might consider taking the tram or a taxi.

○ San Sebastián's train station is a 10-minute walk south of the Parte Vieja; most people simply walk to their hotel or take a taxi.

From the Bus Stations

○ Bilbao's main bus station, Intermodal, is west of the centre. You can easily walk to hotels in the new town, but for elsewhere consider a taxi or the metro (the nearest station is San Mamés, 100m or so away).

○ San Sebastián's bus station is 1km southeast of the Parte Vieja, on the east side of the river, below the Renfe train station.

Getting Around

Bilbao Metro

○ Bilbao has a fast and efficient metro system that runs along two separate lines. There are stations at all the main focal points of El Ensanche and Casco Viejo.

○ Tickets cost €1.60 to €1.90 (€0.91 to €1.19 with a Barik card), depending on the number of zones.

Bilbao Tram

○ Bilbao's tram line runs between Basurtu, in the southwest of the city, and the Atxuri train station.

○ Stops include the Intermodal bus station, the Museo Guggenheim Bilbao, and Teatro Arriaga by the Casco Viejo.

○ Tickets cost €1.50 (€0.73 with a Barik card) and need to be validated in the machine next to the ticket dispenser before boarding your tram.

Barik Card

Save money by purchasing a Barik card for €3 at metro vending machines, topping it up with credit (from €5) and using it on Bilbao's metro, tram and bus lines. One card can be used for multiple people, and the card pays for itself after five uses. Single passes can also be purchased from metro machines.

Basque Country Place & Street Names

The vast majority of places in the Basque Country have Basque-language names rather than Spanish (Castilian) ones (for example, Gernika rather than Guernica). A few places, however, retain Spanish as the primary spelling, the most notable being Bilbao (Basque: Bilbo) and San Sebastián (Basque: Donostia).

Street names in larger cities, towns and villages in the Basque Country use both Spanish and Basque. The street name is preceded by the Spanish, and followed by the Basque, for example 'Calle Correo Kalea' (*calle* is Spanish for 'street', while *kalea* is Basque for 'street'). In small villages, street names are sometimes only in Basque.

Bus

o Not many tourists use the city buses in either Bilbao or San Sebastián. However, bus 16 provides a painless way of getting from San Sebastián city centre to the base of Monte Igueldo via Playa de la Concha.

o Tickets cost €1.80 (€2.10 at night); you can pay the driver directly.

Car

o If you're simply staying put in Bilbao or San Sebastián then forget about hiring a car. It will cost a lot in parking fees and you won't need it in either city.

o If, however, you're planning on making a number of day trips, a car is a godsend as inter-city buses and trains can be irregular.

o There are numerous underground car parks in both cities plus metered parking (expect to pay upwards of €25 for a full day).

o Parking in San Sebastián in summer can be virtually impossible, even at parking stations.

o City hotels generally charge for parking spots.

Taxi

o Taxis in both Bilbao and San Sebastián are only available by reservation or at designated ranks; you can't hail them in the street.

o In Bilbao, try Teletaxi (☎944 10 21 21; www.teletaxibilbao.com).

o In San Sebastián, try Taxi Donosti (☎943 46 46 46; www.taxidonosti.com).

o Expect to pay around €10 to cross central Bilbao or San Sebastián. Rates rise after dark.

Essential Information

Accessible Travel

Most sights in both Bilbao and San Sebastián are wheelchair accessible. However, many cheaper hotels are not. More expensive hotels will have wheelchair accessible rooms.

Business Hours

The following opening hours are common throughout the region.

Banks 8.30am to 2pm Monday to Friday; some also open 4pm to 7pm Thursday and 9am to 1pm Saturday

Nightclubs Midnight or 1am to 5am or 6am

Post Offices 8.30am to 2.30pm & 4.30pm to 8pm Monday to Friday, 9.30am to 1pm Saturday

Restaurants Lunch 1pm to 4pm, dinner 8.30pm to 11pm or midnight

Shops 10am to 2pm and 4.30pm to 7.30pm or 5pm to 8pm; big supermarkets and department stores generally open 10am to 10pm Monday to Saturday

Discount Cards

o Bilbao's **Artean Pass** (adult €17) covers the Museo Guggenheim Bilbao and the Museo de Bellas Artes, and offers significant savings. It's available at both museums.

o The **Bilbao Bizkaia Card** (24/48/72 hours €10/15/20) entitles the user to free citywide transport, free guided tours offered by the tourist office and reductions at many sights. It can be purchased from any of the Bilbao tourist offices.

o The **San Sebastián Card** entitles users to free citywide transport, reduced admission rates at many sights, and discounts at various shops, restaurants and tour operators. Cards are valid for 10 days, cost €9 or €16 (for six or 12 trips on public transport; night trips count as two rides), and are available at the tourist office.

Electricity

Type C
220V/50Hz

Type F
230V/50Hz

Money

The currency in Spain is the euro (€).

ATMs

ATMs are widely available in both cities, but fewer and further between on the Central Basque Coast.

Credit Cards

Credit cards are accepted in most hotels, restaurants and shops; Visa and Mastercard are the most prevalent.

Exchanging Money

Banks and building societies offer the best

exchange rates; take your passport.

Tipping

Bars It's rare to leave a tip in bars (even if the bartender gives you your change on a small dish).

Restaurants Many locals leave small change, others up to 5%, which is considered generous.

Taxis Optional, but most locals round up to the nearest euro.

Public Holidays

Many shops are closed and many attractions operate on reduced hours on the following dates:

Año Nuevo (New Year's Day) 1 January

Epifanía/Día de los Reyes Magos (Epiphany/Three Kings' Day) 6 January

Jueves Santo (Maundy/Holy Thursday) March/April

Viernes Santo (Good Friday) March/April

Fiesta del Trabajo (Labour Day) 1 May

Día de Santiago Apóstol (Feast of St James the Apostle) 25 July

La Asunción (Feast of the Assumption) 15 August

Fiesta Nacional de España (National Day) 12 October

Día de Todos los Santos (All Saints Day) 1 November

Día de la Constitución (Constitution Day) 6 December

La Inmaculada Concepción (Feast of the Immaculate Conception) 8 December

Navidad (Christmas) 25 December

Safe Travel

○ The Basque Country is generally very safe, with few visitors experiencing any major problems.

○ In Bilbao, the area just south of the old town across the river, especially on and around Calle de San Francisco, can be seedy day and night.

○ Petty theft is relatively rare in the region, but stay alert for pickpockets.

○ Cars, especially those belonging to tourists, are a particular target at beaches. Don't leave *anything* of value in your vehicle.

Money-Saving Tips

Many restaurants offer a lunchtime *menú del día*. These mutli-course meals, which typically cost from €10 to €13, are a great way to eat well on a budget.

○ The Basque Country is serious surf country and many beaches are plagued by dangerous undertows and large waves. Always swim in the designated swimming areas and obey lifeguards' instructions.

○ ETA-related terrorism is, hopefully, a thing of the past, but political protests remain common and these can occasionally turn violent. If you encounter a political protest, it's best to avoid any involvement.

○ Find out the latest COVID-19 guidelines before you travel on Spain's Ministry of Health's website (www.mscbs.gob.es/en). For local requirements in the Basque Country, check www.euskadi.eus.

Dos & Don'ts

o Do greet people with *Kaixo* ('hello' in Basque) and farewell them with *Agur* (goodbye); some words of Basque are greatly appreciated.

o Alternatively use the Spanish *Hola* (hello) or *Adiós* (goodbye).

o Do greet friends and family with a kiss on each cheek, or shake hands with strangers if offered.

o Don't talk politics, and definitely don't talk Basque politics unless you really know your stuff.

Toilets

o Public toilets aren't all that common in either Bilbao or San Sebastián, though some exist around the beach area and down by the port in San Sebastián.

o Another option is to use the toilets in a large shopping centre.

o If you go into a bar or restaurant to use a toilet, it's good form to buy a drink as well.

Tourist Information

Bilbao

Main Tourist Office
(944 79 57 60; www.bilbaoturismo.net; Plaza Circular 1; 9am-8pm;) The very helpful main branch of the tourist office is near the Abando train station.

Tourist Office (www.bilbaoturismo.net; Alameda Mazarredo 66; 10am-7pm Jul-Aug, to 3pm Sun Sep-Jun) Useful info point right outside the Guggenheim.

Tourist Office (944 03 14 44; www.bilbaoturismo.net; Bilbao Airport; 9am-9pm) Gives info on Bilbao and the whole Basque region.

San Sebastián

Oficina de Turismo
(943 48 11 66; www.sansebastianturismo.com; Alameda del Boulevard 8; 9am-8pm Mon-Sat, 10am-7pm Sun Jul-Sep, 9am-7pm Mon-Sat, 10am-2pm Sun Oct-May) This friendly office offers comprehensive information on the city and the Basque Country in general.

Visas

o Citizens or residents of EU and Schengen countries don't require a visa.

o From 1 January 2021, non-EU nationals who don't require a visa for entry to the Schengen area need prior authorisation to enter under the new European Travel Information and Authorisation System (ETIAS; www.etias.com).

o Travellers can apply online; the cost is €7 for a three-year, multi-entry authorisation.

o Nationals of other countries should check with a Spanish embassy or consulate about applying for a Schengen visa.

Responsible Travel

Top tips for travelling responsibly:

o Leave a light footprint: take public transport, walk or cycle. In addition to bike-rental companies, the two cities have shared-bike schemes: Bilbaobizi (www.bilbaobizi.bilbao.eus/en/bilbao) in Bilbao and Dbizi (www.dbizi.eus) in San Sebastián.

○ Stay in eco-friendly accommodation: check properties' environmental policies (eg reducing water usage and packaging) and certification (such as the EU Ecolabel).

○ Eat sustainably: pick up ingredients for a picnic or self-catering meal at produce markets or small, specialised food and/or drink shops where you'll find every-thing from cheeses to chocolates, craft beers and the region's traditional ciders, and choose one of the numerous restaurants and bars serving bite-size pintxos featuring seasonal, locally sourced produce.

○ Support local creators and businesses: in Bilbao, browse for locally made design at DendAZ, Basque berets at Gorostiaga, and bags made from recycled materials at Rzik; in San Sebastián, try crafts from Alboka Artesanía and Basque musical instruments from Erviti.

○ Embrace Basque culture: catch cultural festivals, events and performances, and use at least a few words of Euskara (the Basque language) when interacting with locals, such as mesedez (please) and eskerrik asko (thank you).

○ Help counter overtourism: travel outside high summer if possible (April to June, September and October are quieter and cheaper); keep noise down to avoid disturbing residents' sleep; and visit key sights outside peak hours and consider under-the-radar alternatives.

Language

Spanish (*español*) – often referred to as *castellano* (Castilian) to distinguish it from other languages spoken in Spain – is the most widely understood language across the country. Basque (*euskara*) is spoken in the Basque country (*el país vasco*) and is one of the four official languages of Spain. Speaking Spanish in Basque speaking cities such as Bilbao and San Sebastián will generally be expected from a foreigner. Travellers who learn a little Spanish should be relatively well understood.

Most Spanish sounds are pronounced the same as their English counterparts. Just read our pronunciation guides as if they were English and you'll be understood. Note that 'm/f' indicates masculine and feminine forms.

To enhance your trip with a phrasebook, visit lonelyplanet.com.

Basics

Hello.
Hola.　　　　　　　o·la

Goodbye.
Adiós.　　　　　　　a·dyos

How are you?
¿Qué tal?　　　　　ke tal

Fine, thanks.
Bien, gracias.　　　byen gra·thyas

Please.
Por favor.　　　　　por fa·vor

Thank you.
Gracias.　　　　　　gra·thyas

Excuse me.
Perdón.　　　　　　per·don

Sorry.
Lo siento.　　　　　lo syen·to

Yes./No.
Sí./No.　　　　　　see/no

Do you speak (English)?
¿Habla (inglés)?　　a·bla (een·gles)

I (don't) understand.
Yo (no) entiendo.　yo (no) en·tyen·do

Eating & Drinking

I'm a vegetarian. (m/f)
Soy　　　　　　　soy
vegetariano/a.　　ve·khe·ta·rya·no/a

Cheers!
¡Salud!　　　　　　sa·loo

That was delicious!
¡Estaba　　　　　es·ta·ba
buenísimo!　　　　bwe·nee·see·mo

Please bring the bill.
Por favor nos　　　por fa·vor nos
trae la cuenta.　　tra·e la kwen·ta

I'd like ...
Quisiera ...　　　kee·sye·ra ...

a coffee　　*un café*　　oon ka·fe

a table　　*una mesa*　oo·na me·sa
for two　　*para dos*　pa·ra dos

a wine　　　*un vino*　　oon vee·no

two beers　*dos*　　　　dos
　　　　　　cervezas　ther·ve·thas

Shopping

I'd like to buy ...
Quisiera
kee·*sye*·ra
comprar ...
kom·*prar* ...

May I look at it?
¿Puedo verlo?
pwe·do ver·lo

How much is it?
¿Cuánto cuesta?
kwan·to *kwes*·ta

That's too/very expensive.
Es muy caro.   es
mooy *ka*·ro

Emergencies

Help!
¡Socorro!
so·*ko*·ro

Call a doctor!
¡Llame a
lya·me a oon
un médico!
me·*dee*·ko

Call the police!
¡Llame a
lya·me a
la policía!   la
po·lee·*thee*·a

I'm lost. (m/f)
Estoy perdido/a.
es·*toy* per·*dee*·do/a

I'm ill. (m/f)
Estoy enfermo/a.
es·*toy* en·*fer*·mo/a

Where are the toilets?
¿Dónde están
don·de es·*tan*
los baños?   los
ba·nyos

Time & Numbers

What time is it?
¿Qué hora es?   ke
o·ra es

It's (10) o'clock.
Son (las diez).   son
(las dyeth)

morning   *mañana*
ma·*nya*·na

afternoon   *tarde*
tar·de

evening   *noche*
no·che

yesterday   *ayer*
a·*yer*

today   *hoy*
oy

tomorrow   *mañana*
ma·*nya*·na

1	*uno*	oo·no
2	*dos*	dos
3	*tres*	tres
4	*cuatro*	*kwa*·tro
5	*cinco*	*theen*·ko
6	*seis*	seys
7	*siete*	*sye*·te
8	*ocho*	o·cho
9	*nueve*	*nwe*·ve
10	*diez*	dyeth

Transport & Directions

Where's ...?
¿Dónde está ...?
don·de es·*ta* ...

What's the address?
¿Cuál es la   kwal
es la
dirección?
dee·rek·*thyon*

Can you show me (on the map)?
¿Me lo puede   me
lo *pwe*·de
indicar
een·dee·*kar*
(en el mapa)?   (en
el *ma*·pa)

I want to go to ...
Quisiera ir a ...
kee·*sye*·ra eer a ...

What time does it arrive/leave?
¿A qué hora   a ke o·ra
llega/sale?   *lye*·ga/*sa*·le

I want to get off here.
Quiero bajarme
kye·ro ba·*khar*·me
aquí.   a·*kee*

Behind the Scenes

Send Us Your Feedback

We love to hear from travellers – your comments help make our books better. We read every word, and we guarantee that your feedback goes straight to the authors. Visit **lonelyplanet.com/contact** to submit your updates and suggestions.

Note: We may edit, reproduce and incorporate your comments in Lonely Planet products such as guidebooks, websites and digital products, so let us know if you don't want your comments reproduced or your name acknowledged. For a copy of our privacy policy visit lonelyplanet.com/privacy.

Catherine's Thanks

Eskerrik asko/muchas gracias to Julian, and to all of the locals and fellow travellers in the Basque Country, Navarra and La Rioja who provided insights, information and great times. Huge thanks too to Sandie Kestell, Genna Patterson, Darren O'Connell, Tom Stainer and everyone at Lonely Planet. As ever, *merci surtout* to my family.

Acknowledgements

Cover photo: (front) Playa de la Concha and Monte Igueldo, ksl / Shutterstock ©, (back) Basque *pintxos* in a San Sebastián bar, Alexandre Rotenberg / Shutterstock ©

This Book

This 3rd edition of Lonely Planet's Pocket *Bilbao & San Sebastián* was researched and written by Catherine Le Nevez. The previous editions were written and researched Regis St Louis, Stuart Butler and Duncan Garwood. This guidebook was produced by the following:

Senior Product Editor Sandie Kestell

Product Editors Paul Harding, Ross Taylor

Assisting Editors Will Allen, James Bainbridge, Peter Cruttenden

Cartographers Corey Hutchison, Valentina Kremenchutskaya, Anthony Phelan

Book Designers Brooke Giacomin, Aomi Ito

Cover researcher Gwen Cotter, Naomi Parker

Thanks to Darren O'Connell, Sonia Kapoor

Index

Index

Sights 000
Map Pages 000

Shopping

Our Writer

Catherine Le Nevez

Catherine's wanderlust kicked in when she road-tripped across Europe from her Parisian base aged four, and she's been hitting the road at every opportunity since, travelling to some 60 countries and completing her Doctorate of Creative Arts in Writing, Masters in Professional Writing, and postgr qualifications in Editing and Publishing along the way. Over the past decade-and-a-half she's written scores of Lonely Planet guides and articles covering Paris, France, Europe and far beyond. Her work has also appeared in numerous online and print publica tions. Topping Catherine's list of travel tips is to tra without any expectations.

Published by Lonely Planet Global Limited
CRN 554153
3rd edition – June 2022
ISBN 978 1 78701 617 0
© Lonely Planet 2022 Photographs © as indicated 2022
10 9 8 7 6 5 4 3 2 1
Printed in Singapore